COMPUTER LITERACY

Second Edition

Richard T. Christoph
Glenn T. Smith

James Madison University

Regents/Prentice Hall
Englewood Cliffs, NJ 07632

Library of Congress Cataloging-in-Publication Data

Computer Literacy/Learn PC
     p.   cm.
     Includes index.
     ISBN 0-13-010844-8
      1. Computer literacy,   2. Microcomputers,   I. Learn PC (Firm)
QA76.9.CG4C64   1993   92-41545
004--dc20   CIP

Acquisition editors: Ted Werthman/Debra Weinberger

Development/production editor: Deborah Brennan
Production editor: Barbara Martinne
Interior designer: Daniel Will-Harris
Illustrator: Freddy Flake
Photo Editor: Lori Morris
Photo Research: Terri Stratford
Cover designer: Rosemarie Paccione

Prepress buyer: Ilene Levy
Manufacturing buyer: Ed O'Dougherty
Scheduler: Leslie Coward

 © 1993 by Regents/Prentice Hall
A Simon & Schuster Company
Englewood Cliffs, New Jersey 07632

Printed in the United States of America

10   9   8   7   6   5   4   3   2   1

ISBN 0-13-010844-8

Prentice Hall International (UK) Limited, *London*
Prentice Hall of Australia Pty. Limited, *Sydney*
Prentice Hall Canada Inc., *Toronto*
Prentice Hall Hispanoamericana, S.A., *Mexico*
Prentice Hall of India Private Limited, *New Delhi*
Prentice Hall of Japan, Inc., *Tokyo*
Simon & Schuster Asia Pte. Ltd., *Singapore*
Editora Prentice Hall do Brasil, Ltda., *Rio de Janeiro*

PHOTO CREDITS

Lesson 1

page 2 top left, courtesy IBM; top right, courtesy Apple Computer; bottom left, courtesy Hewlett-Packard Company; bottom right, courtesy IBM; page 4, courtesy NCR; page 7 top left, courtesy Apple Computer; top right, courtesy Epson America Inc.; bottom left, courtesy Hewlett Packard Company; bottom middle, courtesy Panasonic Communications & Systems Co.; bottom right, courtesy Epson America Inc.; page 8, Paul Shambroom/courtesy Cray Computers; page 9 top, courtesy ETA Systems; bottom, courtesy IBM; page 10 left, courtesy Apple Computer; page 10 right, courtesy IBM, page 12 top, courtesy IBM; bottom, Charles Gupton/Stock, Boston.

Lesson 2

page 26 top, courtesy Wacom; bottom, courtesy IBM; page 29 left, courtesy The Complete PC; right, courtesy Apple Computers; page 29, courtesy Federal Express.

Lesson 3

page 38, courtesy Intelligent Instrumentation Inc.; page 39, courtesy IBM; page 42, Dell Computer; page 49 left, courtesy IBM; right, courtesy Intel; page 50 left, courtesy IBM; right, courtesy Intel; page 51 top, courtesy Apple Computers; bottom left, Apple Computers, bottom middle, Apple Computers; bottom right, Apple Computers.

Lesson 4

page 59, courtesy Micro Display Systems, Inc.; page 67, courtesy Hewlett-Packard Company; page 68, courtesy Hewlett-Packard Company; page 71, courtesy Summa Graphics Corporation; page 72, courtesy IBM.

Lesson 5

page 89, courtesy IBM; page 90, courtesy IBM, page 91, courtesy IBM.

Lesson 6

page 103, courtesy Hayes.

Lesson 8

page 141, courtesy Harnischfeger Engineers, Inc.

TABLE OF CONTENTS

3 THE SYSTEM AND CENTRAL PROCESSING UNITS **37**

4 OUTPUT DEVICES **57**

5

DATA AND STORAGE DEVICES **79**

6

COMMUNICATING WITH OTHER COMPUTERS **99**

Preface

We are currently living in a world where computers and computer systems are pervasive. These computer systems are intertwined with every facet of our life. From the ringing of our electronic alarm clocks in the morning to the singing of the national anthem as the TV goes off the air at night, computers have been involved in our every movement.

It has been projected that by the turn of the century, there will be a microcomputer in one out of every two households in the nation. To make use of these computers and to make intelligent buying decisions, you need to be *computer literate.* To obtain and hold a satisfying job in the next century will require some amount of computer skills and computer literacy. To be involved in discussions with your colleagues and the people around you, you will need to know some of the basic computer terminology and be computer literate.

We feel there are several components of computer literacy. The first component is understanding what computers do and how they can be used to improve your everyday life, both at home and at work. The next component involves knowing generally how computers perform their tasks. Another component involves knowing what equipment is available for various computer systems and deciding what is best for a given need. The final component involves understanding what types of programs are available to help you perform a certain job.

You do not need to know every detail of every component, but you do need to be aware of every component. In a world where computers affect every aspect of your life, being functionally literate also means being computer literate.]

LEARN PC Computer Literacy Video Series

LEARN PC and Regents/Prentice Hall are working closely to bring you the best in instructional materials. The Learn PC Computer Literacy Video Series includes:

- **LEARN PC Computer Literacy Videotape Library**. A library of three videotapes which present a broad range of personal computer concepts and terminology. The first tape is designed to accompany Lesson One. It explains the Input-Output-Processing cycle and shows computers at work. The second tape deals with computer hardware and consists of five lessons. There is one lesson on the tape for each of the five lessons on hardware; input, process, output, storage, and telecommunications.

  The final tape in the series is about software. The first lesson on the tape is designed as a companion to Lessons Seven and Eight in the text. The final lesson on this tape introduces you to running a demonstration program that is included with the tapes.

- **LEARN PC Computer Literacy Student Guidebook.** Provides more extensive coverage of the materials presented in the videotapes.

- **Instructor's Guide**. Contains teaching tips and instructions for using Learn PC video courseware in the classroom or in a self-paced environment. The instructor's guide also contains several tests to measure a student's comprehension of the material.

- **Learning Activity Packets**. Provide step-by-step instructions for students learning in a self-paced environment. A master set is provided free to instructors upon adoption.

Focus of the Computer Literacy Course

The focus of this course is on hardware and software. These are the two components that most directly affect the ordinary citizen. With a firm understanding of hardware terminology and the equipment available, you can make better, more informed buying decisions. With an understanding of the types of software available and what each type of software can do, you will become a better computer consumer and a better computer user.

This course will also focus on microcomputers. Although many users may need to understand the larger mainframe computer systems, most will be more directly involved with microcomputers. For the average citizen, the use of a microcomputer and microcomputer software will be an eventual necessity.

Intended Audience

This course is intended for the general computer user and the consumer. There is no attempt made in this course to satisfy the needs of any particular discipline or profession. This is an introductory text for anyone that wants to understand more about computers in general and microcomputers in particular. It is intended to provide an overview of microcomputer hardware and software. It should be completed before attempting other, more advanced courses in computer systems.

Learning Environment

This course is being used successfully in both instructor-led and self-paced environments for credit and non-credit courses. The Instructor's Guide provides several examples of how the materials can be used to fit your learning environments.

Organization of the Course

Computer Systems In Use
Lesson One provides an overview of the Input-Processing-Output cycle that is at the heart of computer systems. This lesson also introduces you to the use of computer systems in society. This lesson sets the tone for the remainder of the text.

The Input-Process-Output Cycle
The input-processing-output cycle is a fundamental principle behind computer processing. The organization of the text is based upon this fundamental principle. **Lesson Two** identifies the types of input available and the equipment used to input the data into the computer. **Lesson Three** introduces you to the processing step of the cycle and explains

the principles behind the computer processor. **Lesson Four** identifies the types of output available and the equipment used to produce output.

Storage and Telecommunications

The fourth hardware component of a basic computer system is storage. After data has been input, processed, and output, it must be stored. **Lesson Five** explains the principles behind storage and equipment used to store data.

Telecommunication is the link between your computer and the rest of the world. The increase in the use of telecommunication and computer networks has become so dominant on computer systems that it has been included as a necessary component in a basic computer system. **Lesson Six** explains the principles of telecommunications networks.

Software

No computer system is functionally complete until you have programs or software. These programs allow the computer equipment to work together. **Lesson Seven** introduces you to the *system* software used to make the computer system work. **Lesson Eight** introduces you to a variety of *application* software that allows you to accomplish your individual tasks.

Self-Test and Answers

Each lesson is concluded with a set of short review questions designed to test the knowledge learned in the lesson. Answers to the odd-numbered questions can be found at the back of the text.

Acknowledgements

Any project takes a tremendous amount of help from many people. Some of the help is active, other help is passive. We would like to thank everyone involved in this project, many of whom we have never met or spoken with. In particular, we would like to thank the following:

Ted Werthman, Regents/Prentice Hall, the originator of the project and our editor. Thanks for all the active guidance and constructive criticism you have given on this project and others. We are indebted to you for keeping us moving and on schedule.

Debra Weinberger, Regents/Prentice Hall, for the constructive criticism you have given on this project.

Debbie Brennan, Regents/Prentice Hall, for layout and typesetting. It has been a pleasure working with you. Thanks for being an active member of the team. Great job!

Kay Lafleur and Lynne Johnson, Learn PC, for videotape preparation. From the results of the videos, it is apparent that you are professionals and experts at what you do. Thanks for allowing us to actively work with you.

Orinda Christoph and Terri Smith, our wives. Your passive role has been most important to us. Thanks for sacrificing the time that belonged to you while we completed this project. We love you!

George and Erica Christoph, Wes and Jake Smith, our children. Sometimes we wish your role had been more passive, but we understand your needs. With this one completed, we are back with you.

Computing Fundamentals

Learning Objectives

- Define computer literacy.

- State why you should become computer literate.

- Describe hardware and software.

- Identify two input components of a computer.

- Specify the part of the computer that does the processing.

- Name two output devices used by the computer.

- Define four different sizes of computers.

- Identify three responsibilities of using computers.

C omputers have become a part of our daily lives from the checkout counter of the neighborhood grocery store to the local auto repair shop. These computers make our lives much easier and perform an incredible variety of tasks.

Who Uses Computers?

During the past decade, increasing computer usage has had an impact on almost every occupation. Engineers use computers to analyze the stress points of a new bridge under construction. Hotels use the computer for billing and to keep track of room reservations. The auto repair center uses computers to assist in diagnostic evaluations of auto repairs. Computers are also common in the home where they track household finances, access libraries of information, and provide hours of entertainment.

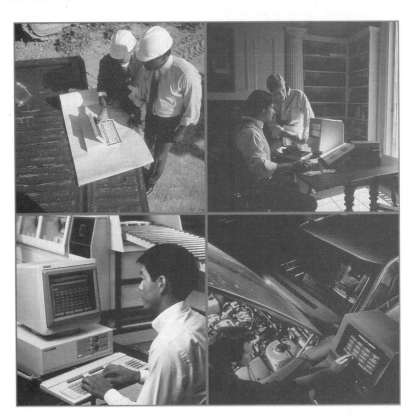

Computers are an essential in many jobs

Today just about everyone is involved with the use of a computer in one way or another, and it is almost certain that you will be involved with computers in your occupation. Computers are powerful tools that can perform many tasks, but, like all tools, you need to know how to use them to get the best results.

What Is Computer Literacy?

Computer literacy is a term that describes the competency level of a person who can use a computer. Literacy in this case means much the same thing as it does when describing a person that can read a book. A person does not have to be an author to be able to read and be literate. Similarly, a computer user does not have to know all the details about the computer; rather, he or she needs only to understand basic concepts about computers to be computer literate.

Computers differ dramatically in power and functions. Part of being computer literate is knowing enough about computers to be able to select the correct computer for the job at hand. A computer that you purchase for home use will likely fulfill different needs when compared to a system that is used in an automotive design studio. Still, you will learn that each computer has the same basic components and functions in much the same way regardless of the size and complexity of the computer.

Reasons to Become Computer Literate

There are many good reasons to become computer literate, but perhaps the most important reason is that your occupation will demand it. Most firms now expect their employees to understand basic computer functions, so being computer literate will provide you with a significant advantage when looking for a job or promotion. In this respect, computer literacy is a necessary part of a person's working life.

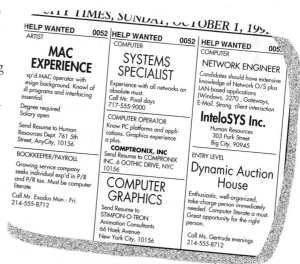

A second reason to become computer literate is to learn enough about computers to be able to buy the correct model for your firm or home. Computers come in many configurations, and it is easy to buy the wrong machine if you are not computer literate. You will also want an idea of what a computer can do in the future so that your purchase will be appropriate for the long run.

Students, regardless of age, are finding that the computer is an indispensable tool. With word processing abilities such as spelling and grammar checking, students are able to write better papers quicker than ever before. Computers can also be connected to each other so that a student has access to libraries of information from a dorm room.

Finally, you should realize that even if your job is one of the few that does not require computer use now, it likely will in the near future. By learning about computer literacy now, you will be prepared to take advantage of opportunities as they appear.

What Is a Computer?

Modern computers appear to be complex and baffling devices but the basic concepts that are used are simple to understand. The fundamental reason that people use a computer is to access *information*. Information can be in the form of a word processing document or a picture to be used in a presentation, but it is still treated by the computer in a similar manner. In fact, all computers follow three basic steps when processing information: Input, Processing, Output. A good example of this sequence is to think of a grocery checkout scanner. When the cashier scans

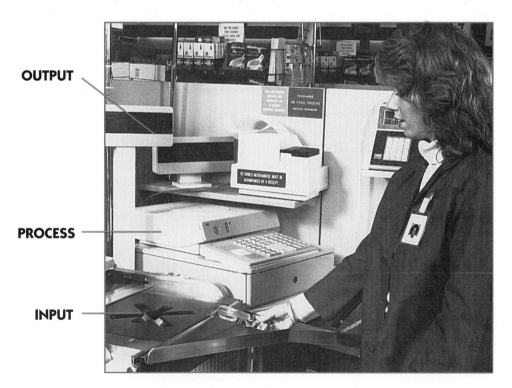

OUTPUT

PROCESS

INPUT

the bar code on the product, the bar code is **input** into the computerized cash register. The computer then **processes** the bar code information to determine the appropriate price of the item. Finally, the price is **output** on the register display.

A computer is a system in which several components work together to input, process, and output information. Two main components of the computer that work together are the *hardware* and *software*. The term hardware refers to the physical machinery of the computer which includes those items that you can see, feel, and touch. Software includes programs which are instructions that tell the computer what to do. We will look at both of these important topics in more depth throughout this book, but let's first begin with a quick overview of hardware and how it works to input, process, and output information.

Input Devices

The Keyboard

Information must be put into the computer before the computer can act upon it in any way, a process which is called input. There are many different methods of inputting data, but the most common is through the keyboard. Keyboards come in many different styles, but they share several common attributes. The computer keyboard looks and operates much like a standard typewriter keyboard and includes the standard 26 letters of the alphabet, the 10 digits used for numbers, and some special characters such as the @ # $ % & * ( ) ?. Lesson 2 will provide more information about many of the special keys that are used on computer keyboards.

The Mouse

A *mouse* is a special desktop device that is used to move the cursor (the pointer on the computer screen) around on the display screen and to select options from screen menus. On the bottom of the mouse is a small ball that rolls when the mouse is moved. As the ball rolls, it causes a signal to be sent to the computer, which moves the pointer or cursor (an arrow on the screen) in the direction that the mouse is moved. The mouse usually has two buttons. By pressing one of these buttons, you can instruct the computer to perform some action where the cursor is resting. Many programs make extensive use of the mouse to select tasks from a computer menu or to draw pictures on the computer screen.

Micro-mouse

The System Unit

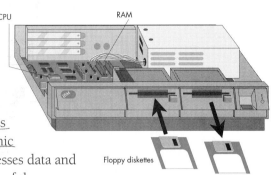

The system unit is the cabinet to which the keyboard and monitor are connected. Often, the system unit is also used as a base for the display unit. Within the system unit is the *central processing unit* (normally referred to as the CPU) which is a small electronic integrated chip that actually processes data and information. The CPU is the heart of the computer system and is the device that allows the machine to perform many different complex mathematical and logic functions. You will also see one or more *diskette drives* housed in the system unit. These devices allow small, magnetic diskettes to be inserted and removed from the computer. Your computer will probably have a fixed or hard disk located under the cover of the system unit. This disk can store information but cannot be removed like the diskettes. Together, the diskette drives and the hard disk provide a storage area for data to be kept until it is processed by the CPU. This storage is called *secondary storage* since it is used to archive data and information until it is needed by the CPU. There is another type of storage called *primary storage.* Primary storage is the working memory of the computer. It uses electronic chips to store information and is erased when the computer is turned off.

Why Is Secondary Storage Important?

Hard disks and diskettes allow you to store your work and then, at a later time, come back and edit or add to it without having to re-enter the earlier information. This ability saves a tremendous amount of typing or other input time. For example, suppose a report that you wanted to write was similar to an earlier one; why not retrieve the earlier one and modify it? Unless you choose to erase the report, it will remain on your disk for months or even years.

Storage, especially using the hard disk, allows you to load and store software programs until you are ready to use them. These programs instruct the computer to perform word processing, spreadsheet, or other tasks. You will learn about software programs a bit later, but remember that without storage, the computer would not be practical.

Output Devices

Various types of monitors and printers

Computers can receive a wide variety of information from many different input devices, store and process it in many different ways, but the information must still be output before it can be used. Computers offer a wide range of output devices, but the most common is the video display monitor.

The video display monitor normally sits on top of the computer system unit and looks much like a TV screen. It is sometimes called a *cathode ray tube* (CRT), or *video display terminal* (VDT), or simply a monitor and it serves as the standard output device for the computer system. Video displays are available in color and monochrome (black and white or green and white).

Another popular output device is the printer. The least expensive printer is the dot matrix printer which provides good quality output and reasonable speed of printing. The newer laser printer is more expensive but offers excellent print quality and higher print speed when compared to the dot matrix. Monitors, printers, and other output devices are discussed in detail in Lesson 3.

Trends in Computing

The modern computer has been available for some 40 to 50 years but over this time has improved dramatically. Simultaneously, the cost of these ever more powerful machines has decreased rapidly. One of the most significant advances that allowed these amazing changes to occur was the development of the microprocessor. The microprocessor is really an entire computer on one small electronic chip and has enabled new computers to become smaller yet more powerful than ever. These advances have been especially important to the development of new and more powerful CPU chips. It is expected that this trend of having increasingly powerful computers at ever decreasing prices will continue and make the computer even more popular in the future than it is today.

Types of Computers

While this course will focus most of its attention on the personal or microcomputer, it is important that you realize there are three other types of computers that are larger and more powerful than the microcomputer. The most powerful computer is the supercomputer, followed by the mainframe, minicomputer, and finally the microcomputer.

Supercomputers

A supercomputer

Supercomputers are the fastest and most powerful computers ever built and they cost many millions of dollars. These computers can perform billions of calculations per second and are used for the most intensive processing requirements. Supercomputers are used to manipulate the massive amounts of data to develop complex mathematical models. Not surprisingly, government agencies and universities are primary users of these expensive, powerful computers.

Mainframes

A mainframe computer

Mainframes are large computers used extensively in business for routine computing tasks. These machines range in cost from about one half million to several million dollars and can process many millions of calculations in one second. A mainframe computer is shared by many users and often is used to provide data to microcomputers that are connected to it with telephone lines. This type of connection or network provides you with the ease of use of the microcomputer and the substantial processing capability of the mainframe. Traditionally, mainframes have represented the largest segment of the computer industry, but this is changing with the advent of the microcomputer.

Minicomputers

A minicomputer

As mainframe computers continued to advance, smaller computers costing up to a quarter of a million dollars became available. These smaller systems provided much of the power of the mainframe but in a less costly, easier to operate package. These machines were perfect for use in firms that were too small to justify the expense of a mainframe. With the continuing decrease in price of the mainframes and the increasing power of the microcomputer, many observers feel that the minicomputer will begin to decline in popularity over the next few years.

Microcomputers

Two types of microcomputers (IBM and Macintosh)

The microcomputer or personal computer consists of computers that cost from a few hundred to ten thousand dollars and offer an incredible range of power, size, and features. There are three general groups of microcomputers: desktop, laptop or notebook, and palm size. Desktop systems are the most common and consist of the usual keyboard, system unit, and monitor. Laptop and notebook computers take advantage of new, smaller electronics to provide all of the computer components in a standard notebook-sized package weighing only a few pounds. Finally, palm-sized computers that weigh a few ounces are available, and some can actually accept hand-written commands.

During the development of microcomputers, both Apple and IBM offered different types of computers with the Apple Macintosh and the IBM/PC or Personal Computer. This situation continues today with both types of computers finding a loyal following among users; however, the IBM-compatible computer is now the most popular.

As the IBM/PC became more popular with users, other companies chose to mimic the IBM system with machines called PC compatibles or clones. These clones work in the same way as the IBM systems and are widely available from many different vendors. This wide availability provides you with many options when you are considering the purchase of a computer.

Being Part of the Computer Age

There are many reasons to be part of the exciting world of computers. One of the most important is that you will likely have to be computer literate to succeed in your job. You may even find yourself working at home, connected to the office through your computer. This "electronic cottage" offers both the employee and the firm many benefits by allowing the employee to work in familiar, comfortable surroundings. Further, the expense and time dedicated to commuting to and from work are eliminated. This concept of *telecommuting* allows the employee to use a *modem* to connect his or her computer with the office over telephone lines. Such an arrangement also allows for very flexible hours and many firms report a substantial increase in employee productivity.

It is possible to communicate directly with your computer through the use of a computer network. A network of computers connects all systems together though wires or phone lines enabling users to share information among others on the network. You can send *electronic mail* consisting of a short note or complex report to anyone on the network. By connecting networks together, many employees routinely send information to other workers around the world. A good example of the network concept is the automatic teller machine (ATM) network that provides bank services at sites hundreds of miles from your local bank.

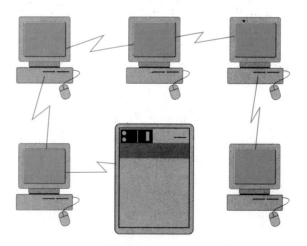

A typical network configuration

Education is also embracing the computer as we strive to remain competitive on a global basis. Preschool children learn to use the computer as a learning tool that reinforces the identification of colors and shapes. Computers allow them to develop their own simple stories through picture identification. This trend continues throughout the educational system where students use the computer to reinforce reading and arithmetic concepts. Students can even access entire encyclopedias available on mainframe computers and accessed through a network.

Finally, you can expect increasing utilization of the computer in your home. Computers will help with your personal finances and tax preparation. You can also connect to commercial networks to access information about sports, financial news, or shopping. People even make their own airline reservations from their computer and send messages to other users around the world.

Computer Responsibilities

Software Piracy

You have learned that the computer is a powerful tool that can provide you with many opportunities. Like any powerful tool, its use carries with it responsibilities. Computer users who would never think of shoplifting a product from a store might be tempted to copy a program for use on their computer without paying for it. This software piracy is the same as any other theft and must be avoided. Many companies make it a practice to discipline or terminate employees that illegally copy programs for their own use. The simple way to avoid this problem is to use only those programs where you have permission from the author to use them. This permission comes in the form of a license for use and is most often obtained by purchasing the program from the software developer or retail outlet.

Computer Privacy

When you use a computer in your work, remember that some of the information you deal with may be confidential, and its release could cause others harm. For this reason, don't leave documents or diskettes lying around where others can access them. Also, be careful when entering or changing data that is stored on the computer. Most of us have experienced the frustrating process of fixing something that has been input incorrectly into the computer. If in doubt, be sure to ask for clarification.

Computer Viruses

You have probably heard a great deal about computer viruses which, like human viruses, can cause your computer to malfunction. The result of virus infections can range from harmless messages which appear on the screen to the destruction of data and programs. Most viruses are transmitted from computer to computer through the copying and sharing of programs either by diskette or though the use of a telephone line. You can prevent most potential virus infections by not accepting pirated (illegally copied) software and only connecting to reputable communications networks. A further step is available in the form of virus protection software which will detect and erase the virus from your computer without harming your data. These inexpensive programs can be good insurance and should be used if you need to exchange data diskettes with others or connect to many different computer networks.

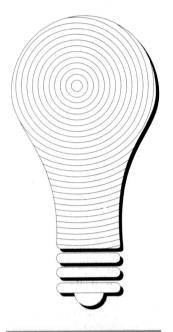

Summary

What is Computer Literacy?

- Computer literacy is a required skill in many occupations and will continue to increase in importance in the future.

- To attain computer literacy, you will need to know how the computer inputs, processes, and outputs information.

- Information is processed using input devices such as the keyboard, processed by the Central Processing Unit located in the system unit, and outputted with devices such as the monitor and printer. The computer uses disk and diskette storage to store information until it is needed by the CPU.

What Types of Computers Are Available?

- Computers range in size, price, and performance.

- The smallest computer is the microcomputer or personal computer which is available in the standard desktop model as well as in notebook and palm-sized configurations.

- Larger, more powerful computers include the minicomputer, mainframe computer, and super computer. These larger computers are used to perform processing for an entire firm or to compute sophisticated mathematical models.

Responsibilities Of Using Computers

- You should recognize that with the use of the computer comes responsibility.

- An important ethical responsibility is not to steal software by copying it without paying for it.

- Much of the information on the computer will be confidential and you must not allow others to use your computer without authorization.

- Recognize that although unlikely, a computer virus infection is possible. Guard against this by not sharing diskettes with other users and connecting to responsible information services. Consider purchasing an inexpensive virus protection program which will protect your computer against a virus attack.

Review Questions

Answer the following questions to check your understanding of the lesson material.

1. Who uses computers today?

2. Define computer literacy.

3. What are three important reasons for you to become computer literate?

4. The computer allows users to access _____.

5. What are the three fundamental processing steps all computers utilize?

6. When the computer is used, both _____ and _____ must work together.

7. What is the system unit?

8. What are the four major kinds of computers available today?

9. How does telecommuting work?

10. When does software piracy occur?

11. What is a computer virus and how can you protect your computer from it?

Input Devices

Learning Objectives

fixtures you see + touch

commands that tell computer what to do

- Define the terms hardware and software.

- Explain the function of input data and input devices.

- Explain the function of many of the computer keyboard's keys.

- List several (touch) input devices and explain how they work.

- List several (visual) or optical input devices and explain how they work.

- List several (sound) and audio input devices and explain how they work.

- Define the terms: function key, mouse, track ball, scanner, Universal Product Code, MICR, synthesizer, and device driver. — *hardware*

In the next five lessons you will learn about computer hardware. The computer hardware is the devices and the equipment that make up the computer system. Stated simply, if you can touch it, it is computer hardware. You will also see the term software. Software refers to the computer instructions or programs that tell the hardware what to do. You cannot touch the software. Software is discussed in more detail in future lessons.

3. It is important to remember that virtually all hardware devices will require some type of software program in order to work properly. These software programs that control the operation of the hardware are referred to as device drivers. In the following discussions of hardware, a reference to a device driver may not be made, but you should remember that one will be required. The device driver must be compatible with the hardware device it is controlling.

1. In this lesson you will learn about input devices. Input devices are hardware that allow you to enter data or information into the computer. In subsequent lessons you will learn about the processor that allows you to process the data, output devices that allow you to output the processed information, storage devices that allow you to store data and information, and networking and communication devices that allow you to communicate with other computers. Before we examine input devices, we must look at the function of input data.

What Is Input?

Remember that the three primary functions of a computer system are input, process, and output. Before information can be processed and output, the data must be entered into the system. Before it is processed, this data is referred to as the input data. As a review of this input-process-output cycle let's assume you wanted to average three test scores. You must first enter the scores. This would give the computer system some raw data or input with which to work. The processing step would be to add the three scores together and divide the sum of the scores by three. Finally, the output step would be to display the average to you. As you can see, without the input, there would be no data to process and no average to display.

Since the input data is the beginning point for the processing, the output can be no more accurate than the input. For example, if you had entered an incorrect test score in the averaging example above, you would not get your correct test average. The average would be correct for the numbers provided, but it would not be the correct average. This example of bad input data gives us the term GIGO — *garbage in, garbage out.* If you input garbage or incorrect data into the computer system, you should expect garbage or incorrect information as output

---

from the computer system. In fact, the predominate source of errors in a computer system comes from incorrect input.

Input Devices

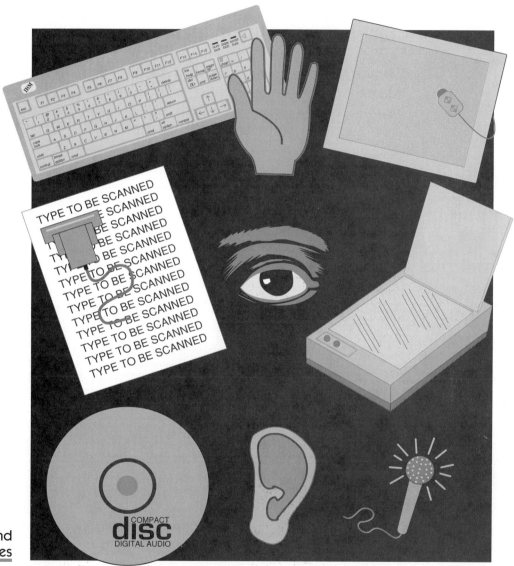

Touch, visual, and audio input devices

Input devices allow you to enter the raw data to be processed into the computer system and are considered computer hardware. The function of any input device is to convert data found in the outside world into an electronic form that can be understood by the computer. For example, when you touch a key on a computer keyboard, the key touched is translated into an electronic image, passed through the processor, and stored in memory. In this lesson we will discuss only the most common devices, but you should remember that there are many other devices which can be used to input data.

Input devices can be divided into three major categories. The first category is touch devices. To enter data from these devices, you must touch the device. The most common *touch* device is the computer keyboard. The second category is *visual* or optical devices. The devices enter data by looking at the raw data, recognizing the image it sees, and translating the image into electronic signals. Common visual devices are cameras and scanners. The third category of devices is *sound* oriented. These devices listen to the sounds and record the sounds into signals. A common sound input device is a microphone. Each category of input device will be discussed in turn.

Touch Input Devices

Computer Keyboard

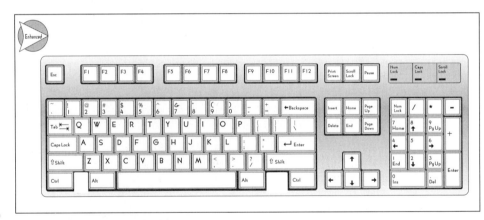

The standard 101
keyboard

4.a.

The simplest and most common input device found on computer systems is the keyboard. The keyboard is used to enter text (words), numbers, and symbols into the computer's memory. The exterior of the keyboard looks and works much like a typewriter keyboard except that there is an electronic circuit board that lies beneath the keys. When a key is pressed, a circuit is connected on this circuit board and an electronic signal is sent to the processor. The processor interprets the signal to determine which key was pressed.

There are many types and styles of computer keyboards. The primary differences among the different types of keyboards are the location of some of the keys, the number of special keys available, and the *touch* and *feel* of the keyboard. The most common type of keyboard is the 101 enhanced keyboard. The 101 keyboard has one hundred and one keys and uses the standard *QWERTY* key layout. This key layout is the same as that of most typewriters and gets its name from the first six keys on the top left part of the keyboard, namely the Q,W,E,R,T, and Y keys.

Most keyboards have a numeric keypad. This keypad is used to allow quick and easy input of numbers. The layout of the numeric keypad is the same as that used on most calculators with the exception that the keys may serve more than one function. For example, on the 101 keyboard's numeric keypad the number **2** key also serves as the *down arrow* key. This means that you may get the number **1** entered or you may move your *cursor* down one line depending upon which mode the keyboard is in. Other keys on the keypad also serve multiple functions.

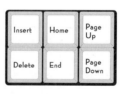

4.b.
The numeric keypad

To force the numeric keypad to enter numbers, rather than its other function, you need to press the **Num Lock**. This key locks the numeric keypad into its number entry mode. When the keypad is in this mode, you will enter numbers rather than use the keypad's other functions. Normally there will be a light on the keyboard to indicate that the key pad is in *Num Lock* mode. To change back to the keypad's other functions, press the **Num Lock** key a second time.

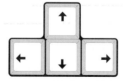

4c.   **The cursor movement keys**

The keyboard also has several cursor movement keys. The *cursor* is a small, flashing light that appears on your computer's screen. It may be a vertical bar, an underline, a small crosshair, or sometimes a small block. Its function is to show

---
Input Devices

you where the information you type will appear. Cursor movement keys allow you to move your cursor to different locations on your computer display screen. For example, the down arrow key will move the cursor down one line, the up arrow key moves the cursor up one line, left and right arrow keys move the cursor left and right. Other cursor movement keys, such as the **Home, End, Page Up** and **Page Down** keys, also move the cursor. Exactly where the cursor moves depends on the particular software program you are using.

4.d.

The function keys

Most keyboards have special function keys. These keys are labeled F1, F2, F3, etc. Function keys, as their names imply, perform special processing functions or operations. The exact function that each key performs depends upon the software program used. For example, the F1 function key may save a file in one program, but it may print a file in a different program. Because of the differences in programs, many programs provide a *template* for the function keys. A template is a small plastic cover or outline of the function keys with an indication of what each function key does.

A keyboard may have the function keys set up vertically on the left hand side of the keyboard, or they may be set up horizontally at the top of the keyboard. A particular keyboard may also have either 10 or 12 function keys depending upon the style of the keyboard. There are some keyboards that have the function keys both on the left and on the right. You may also find keyboards that have more than 12 function keys, but the standard is either 10 or 12.

Other keys to note on the keyboard:

Alt

Alt key: This is the alternate key and is normally used with other keys. When it is used with another key, it changes the function or the character the key represents.

Ctrl

Ctrl key: This is the control key and its use is similar to the ALT key. It is normally used with another key to change the function of the key. The Ctrl key is also used to enter special types of codes that are not represented by keys on the keyboard.

Shift

CapsLock

Shift key and Caps Lock keys: These keys are used to shift the keyboard into upper or lower case characters. The shift key is held down while another key is pressed to get the opposite case (upper or lower). The Caps Lock key locks the keyboard into upper case mode.

Learn PC Computer Literacy

Backspace and Delete keys: These keys are used to erase characters. The Backspace key deletes the character to the left of the cursor; the Delete key deletes the character the cursor is sitting on or the character to the right of the cursor.

Esc key: This is the escape key. It is used to cancel the operation you are currently performing. ←

Enter or Return keys: These keys are used to tell the computer system that you have completed entering data or used to choose a selected option. In essence, they tell the processor to take the data entered and process it.

Most of the keys on the keyboard are *auto-repeat* keys. Auto repeat means that if you hold the key down for several seconds, the character or function of the key will repeat for as long as you have the key pressed.

Some of the things to consider when buying a keyboard are the location and number of function keys, the *touch and feel* of the keyboard, the size of the keyboard (make sure the keys are large enough for your fingers), and the location of the numeric keypad. You can even get keyboards set up for left-handed people. ← ◡

CARE OF THE KEYBOARD

- Protect the keyboard from spills. Spills may short circuit the keyboard or gum up the keys.

- Keep the keyboard away from extremely dusty and polluted areas.

- Clean and vacuum the keyboard frequently.

- Never bang or strike the keyboard with a strong force. Protect the keyboard from falls.

- When not in use, keep the keyboard covered.

Mouse

Another type of touch input device is the *mouse*. The mouse is used as a pointing and selecting device rather than a data entry device. This means that you do not use the mouse to enter data; you use it to position the cursor or to select existing data and options from program menus. To use the mouse, roll it on the desktop. As the mouse moves, it moves the cursor on the

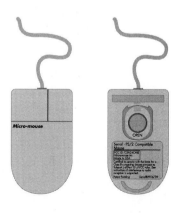

---

screen. A mouse will also require mouse *device driver* software that is compatible with the brand and type of mouse used.

There are several different types and styles of mice. The most common is the mechanical mouse. This type of mouse contains a small ball in the bottom of the mouse. As the mouse is rolled across a desktop, the ball turns a set of rollers inside the mouse. The movement of these rollers sends signals to the processor indicating the direction that the mouse is moved. The mouse is connected to the computer by a small cable that is used to transfer the signals to the processor. This cable is the mouse's tail.

Other types of mice use optical techniques to inform the processor of the mouse's movement. This type of mouse has an infrared beam and a special mouse pad. As the mouse is rolled across the pad, the beam makes contact with grid lines on the pad to indicate the mouse movement. This type of mouse is reputed to be more accurate since it has no internal moving parts.

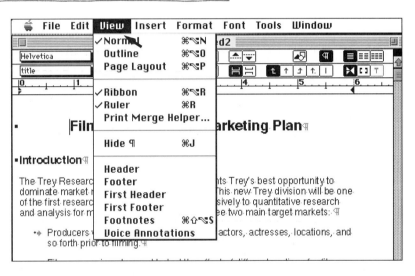

A pull-down menu with the mouse's arrow cursor

Most mice have two buttons. Normally the left button is used to select items on your computer screen. To select items on the screen, you move the mouse's cursor, usually an arrow or a crosshair, to the location you want to select and press the left button. When you press the button, it is referred to as *clicking the mouse*. For example, to select an option from a menu, you might point to the word on the menu and *click* the left button. Sometimes you may need to *double click* the mouse to choose an option. When you double click, you simply press the mouse button twice in rapid succession. One other operation you commonly do with a mouse is to *drag the mouse*. When *dragging* the mouse, position the mouse cursor on an object or area of text and hold the mouse button down while you move the mouse. Dragging allows you to move objects on the screen or select more than one object on the screen.

The operation of the right mouse button and the middle mouse button on three button mice are controlled by mouse control software. This software will allow you to swap the functions of the left and right buttons to make it easier for left handed people to use. The right and middle mouse buttons are also used by some software programs to perform special operations. Check with the software owners information for details on specific software.

A common variation of the mouse is the *track ball*. This device is essentially the same as a mouse turned upside down. Rather than rolling the mouse across the desktop, you use your finger to roll the ball of the track ball in a socket. The advantage of the track ball is that it requires less space on the desktop since the socket that holds the ball does not need to move. There are other variations of the mouse, but the track ball is the most common.

CARE OF THE MOUSE

- On mechanical mice, the mouse ball may build up with dirt or a grease film. To clean the mouse, remove the mouse ball and wash the ball in warm soapy water. Make sure you dry the mouse ball before replacing it in the mouse.

- Use a mouse pad. A mouse pad is a small foam rubber pad usually covered with a fabric coating. This rough fabric coat helps give the mouse ball traction so you get better accuracy and consistent movement when you move the mouse. The mouse pad also decreases the wear on the feet of the mouse.

- Don't tug on the mouse cable. Frequent tugs on the cable can loosen or break the wires in the cable and render the mouse inoperable.

Drawing Pads

Another type of touch input device is the *drawing pad* which uses a special pen and pad. As an image is drawn on the pad, it is transferred into the memory of the computer. Drawing pads are often used by architects, engineers, artists, designers, drafters, and many other professionals where the ability to modify a drawing is important. For example, a graphic artist might use a drawing pad to sketch the design for an advertisement. The designer could then use the computer to add special effects to the drawing, test different colors, rotate the drawing, or combine several drawings together. An architect might sketch the blueprint of a house on a drawing pad, then use the computer to enlarge a room, move a room, or try different window styles on the house.

Touch Screen

Touch screens are input devices that are also output devices. Most touch screens are used to allow a user to choose an option from a menu or to choose a picture from a screen. These screens have special pressure sensitive areas on them. When an area of the screen is touched, the computer software is written to perform a special function depending upon where you touch the screen.

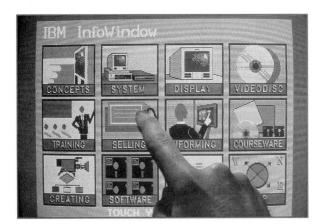

A touch screen

An example of a touch screen might be found in a large shopping mall. You could touch the name of a store, and the computer could highlight the location of the store on a map of the mall. Touch screens are also used in elementary education where one side of the screen displays pictures of several animals and the names of the animals on the other side. The child touches the picture and the corresponding animal name. If they match, the child is rewarded with special sounds or visual effects.

Touch screens are most effectively used when the number of options a user can choose are limited. They can also be effective where language may be a barrier, such as in an international airport where pictures could be used in place of words.

Pen-based Handwriting Pads

Pen-based handwriting pads are among the newer of the touch based input devices. These are devices that use a special pen and writing pad. The user simply writes on the pad, and the handwriting is translated into computer input as it is written. The user can then use computer programs, like word processors, to modify what has been entered. One of the primary problems with pen-based handwriting pads is recognizing the handwriting itself. The user needs to be very careful to write in a style that is recognizable by the machine. These pads help eliminate the duplicated effort of writing a note or document, then retyping the document using the keyboard.

Visual Input Devices

Visual input devices input data by looking at the data, recognizing the data it sees, and converting the image that is recognized into electronic signals that the computer can understand. These devices are commonly referred to as *optical character readers* (OCR) or *optical mark readers* (OMR). The technology of most visual input devices is extremely good with accuracy rates very near 100 percent.

Image Scanners

Image scanners work much like photocopiers in that the scanned figure is stored electronically in the computer's memory. Normally, a light beam is passed over (or under) the image that you want input into the computer system. By using reflected light, the scanner determines the shape of the image it is trying to scan. This image is passed into the computer's memory as a stream of electronic signals. The device *driver* software tells the scanner exactly how to organize the electronic signals for the computer system.

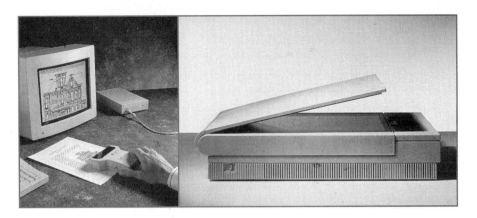

A hand-held and
page scanner

#8.

There are several types of image scanners with the two most common types being page and hand-held scanners. Most page scanners look like small desktop copiers. These scanners input an entire page of graphics or text into the computer at one time. The page to be scanned is placed on the *bed* of the scanner, and the light beam is passed under the page. Some page scanners can input 5 to 6 pages per minute depending upon the type of information being scanned. This type of scanner is relatively expensive, costing from $600 to several thousand dollars, but produces very good results quickly.

The second type of image scanner is a hand-held scanner. With this type of scanner, the user *drags* the scanner across the image or text to be input into the computer. If the image to be scanned is too wide for the scanner head, the image may need to be scanned several times, getting part of the image each time. Hand-held scanners are relatively inexpensive, costing from $200 to $500, but usually do not produce as high a quality image as a page scanner.

Most image scanners can scan both graphics and text. Many scanners can scan and store colors as well. Graphics and pictures are scanned by artists, publishers, designers, and other professionals to help illustrate a document or advertisement. Text or written words are sometimes scanned by many professionals to avoid retyping information from a printed document. The scanned graphics and text can then be combined using other software programs to create catalogs, advertisements, textbooks, or almost anything imaginable. Many businesses and government organizations that are required to keep historical documents are scanning these documents and storing them electronically.

Bar-Code Scanners

Bar-code scanners differ from image scanners in that bar code scanners do not store the image they scan. Rather, these types of scanners recognize the bars that are scanned and convert the bar codes into numbers that are inputted into the computer system. The computer system then works with the numbers rather

---

than the bars themselves. Bar-code scanners can be either hand-held light scanners, like those found in most department stores, or flat-bed laser scanners like those found in most grocery stores.

Bar-code scanners use a standard bar coding system known as the Universal Product Code or UPC. These are the codes that you see on almost every product you buy today. Each bar represents a numeric digit depending upon the bar's width and the space between bars. When the bar-code scanner recognizes the bar, it simply converts the bar to its corresponding digit and sends the digit to the computer system. The computer system then matches the item number read by the scanner to its description, price, and other information that is stored. This other information then can be printed on a sales receipt or other document as output.

A bar code and bar-code scanner

Bar codes can be used anywhere a product needs to be identified. Even the United States Post Office uses bar code readers to track shipments. Accuracy of bar codes and bar-code scanners approach 100 percent. This is surprising when considering all the different sizes, locations, and angles that are used to place the bar codes on products.

Optical-Mark Readers

Mark readers are relatively simple devices when compared to image scanners and bar-code readers. Mark readers simply detect the location of a mark on a form. You have probably used these to take standardized or objective tests.

✗ The technique, used to detect the mark, commonly uses light reflected

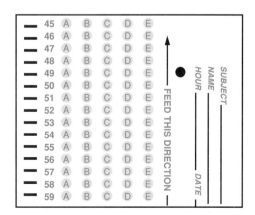

from the graphite in pencil lead. A beam of light is directed at each row or column of the answer sheet. If a pencil mark is present, the graphite in the pencil lead will reflect the light to a photo cell, indicating the presence of the mark. Because the reader is only looking for the reflected light, you must make sure your pencil lead has enough graphite to register and that your erasures are clean. If the lead is too light, the mark may not be detected. If erasures are not clean, or are smeared, the reader may detect a mark in the wrong location thereby detecting an incorrect answer. Since ink does not contain graphite, pens cannot be used to mark this type of form.

Mark readers are used when the volume of input is small and relatively simple. This is the reason why they are good for objective tests. You simply need to indicate a true or false answer or a letter for a multiple choice answer. If the volume of data to be input is large or involves words or text, you should use an image scanner rather than a mark reader.

Magnetic Ink Character Recognition (MICR)

This type of character recognition uses magnetic particles mixed in the ink used to encode the account number on checks and deposit slips. This particular type of input device is used almost exclusively by the banking industry. In fact, this method of encoding checks is required by the Federal Reserve before it will process and forward checks.

Peter X. Pixel
700 Quadra Crash Road
Macintosh, CA 93200

October 1 19 92   426

Pay to the
order of ___Software City Custom Programs___ | $ | 500.02

Five-Hundred-dollars and two cents ——————— ²/₁₀₀ **Dollars**

National Bank of Memory
ASBURY ISLAND, NEW JERSEY

For: Image software Pkg.

⑈620279109⑈ 07648 781⑈ 0921

MICR readers detect the shape of a character based on the pattern of the magnetic particles in the ink. Once the shape of the characters is detected, it is compared to characters that are already stored in the reader's memory. When the reader matches the character it read with one that it has stored, it knows what signals to send to the computer system.

You may have noticed a strip of white tape across the bottom of a check that has been returned from the bank. What has happened is the ink in your account number has been smeared or otherwise been found unreadable. Since the ink is magnetic, it must be taped over so the magnetic particles will not be detected when your account number is re-encoded on the check. Occasionally, you will find this tape below the amount of the check. In this case, the incorrect amount of the check was encoded by the bank teller and must be covered and re-encoded.

Sound or Audio Input Devices

There are also input devices that accept sound. This third category of input device gives the computer three of the same senses you have — touch, sight, and hearing. The two most common sound input devices are *music synthesizers* and *voice recognition systems.*

Music Synthesizers

The first common audio input device is a music synthesizer. These devices record music in a digitized form so that it can be stored electronically. Once the music is recorded electronically, it can be modified in many ways. For example, the computer system could change the *chord* the music is played in from A to B or C. This changes the pitch of the music. It could also be played faster or slower.

Another advantage of having the music recorded electronically in the computer is that you can *cut* and *paste* parts of different recordings. In this way you can create new music from existing pieces. You can also rearrange the music in the same recording. Depending upon the software being used, you may even be able to change the instrument used to play the music.

Voice-recognition Devices

As the name implies, these types of input devices attempt to take spoken words and store them as typed text. Once the voice is stored as text, it can be processed by word processing software or any other software just as if you had entered it from the keyboard.

The basic approach to voice recognition begins by accepting a spoken word or sentence through a microphone connected to the computer. Once the sound waves are captured, they are transformed into a sequence or code understandable by the computer. Next a phonetic model describes what codes may occur for a given sound. Once the codes are determined, a dictionary is searched for the phonetic pronunciation of each word. Next a grammar-checking system is used to determine if the words found make sense. Using information found from the phonetic model, dictionary, and grammar checking system, the computer tries to find the best sequence of words based upon a variety of examples it has stored in its memory. The process is much more sophisticated than what has just been described, but this should give you an idea of what is involved in voice recognition.

9

Voice recognition is probably the most difficult of the input devices to develop. Some of the problems associated with voice recognition include:

1. **Voice inflection:** Different people emphasize different sounds or syllables for emphasis which causes problems for the computer system.

2. **Voice tone and voice changes:** Some people have high voices and others have deep voices. The computer system must be able to interpret the different pitches of these voices. Also, when you have a cold or a sore throat, your voice changes. This possibility must be considered in voice recognition systems.

3. **Local accents:** The accent of someone from Brooklyn, NY is dramatically different than someone from New Orleans, LA. Now, we are trying to get a machine to understand different accents.

4. **Localized words and slang words:** For the system to work well, the words must be stored in a dictionary. This means that the dictionary must be updated constantly with local terms, slang words, and new words.

5. **External noise,** such as radios, background conversation, noisy machinery, etc., may be interpreted as speech.

Voice-recognition systems currently work well for a limited vocabulary. For example, there are many systems that will accept the ten digits in the decimal numbering system. This type of system could allow you to check a credit card number and possibly the amount of the charge. Other systems may allow you to select an option from a menu where the number of options are limited. This gives the system a small range of words to check. These systems are well adapted to work environments where the workers must have their hands freed from the keyboard.

On more sophisticated systems, the recognition system must be *trained* to recognize an individual's voice. To train the system, a user will speak or read a given set of words or phrases to the system. The words and phases are then stored and used to match against the user's voice the next time that user operates the system. These types of systems give the user more flexibility, but can only be used by someone who has trained the system.

Research and development on voice recognition systems is moving at a fast pace and appears to offer considerable promise for the future.

Other Input Devices

There are many other input devices available. A few examples include video-tape devices, devices that input temperature, air speed, amount of light, sensors that measure thickness or liquid depth, etc. In essence, any device that can convert its data into an electronic signal can be converted to an input device for a computer system. Once the data is converted, software must perform the remainder of the processing on the data.

Adding Input Devices to Your Computer

In order for an input device to get its data into the computer, the device must be connected to the computer. In some cases, this connection may be as easy as plugging the device into one of the *ports* in the back of the system unit. *Ports* are discussed in more detail in the following lesson. In other cases you may need to install an *add-on board* or *expansion card*.

Add-on boards and expansion cards are hardware devices that are inserted into *slots* inside the system cabinet. These cards help with transmission of the data from the input device to the processor and memory. In some cases, the expansion card comes with the input device. In other cases, it must be purchased separately. Add-on boards, cards, and slots are covered in more detail in the next lesson.

When purchasing any input device, you should ask the following questions:

1. Are all required cables included?

2. Can I use an existing port that is currently on my computer system or will I need an add-on board or controller card? If an additional board or card is required, is it included with the input device?

3. Is the device driver software for the input device included?

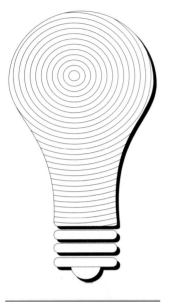

Summary

- <u>Hardware</u> is the equipment of the computer system. You can hold and touch the hardware. <u>Software</u> is the instructions that tell the hardware what to do. You cannot hold or touch the software.

- The function of any <u>input device</u> is to convert data found in the outside world into an electronic form that can be understood by the computer. The input provides data for the processing step of the input-process-output cycle. The output of this cycle can be no more accurate than the input (<u>GIGO</u>).

- The <u>computer keyboard</u> is the most common touch input device. It consists of the character keys, a numeric keyboard, several cursor movement keys, ten or twelve function keys, and several editing keys.

- A <u>mouse</u> is a pointing device used to move your cursor or select items on the screen. Other common <u>touch input devices</u> are the track ball, drawing pad, touch screen, and the pen-based handwriting pad.

- Visual or optical input devices consist of image scanners which are:

  - used in input pictures and text, bar-code readers.

  - used to input Universal Product Codes and other bar shaped codes, mark readers.

  - used to sense the presence of a mark, and magnetic ink readers.

  - used to input data on checks.

- Sound or audio input devices are music synthesizers and voice recognition systems.

- To install an input device on you computer you must have an available port or expansion card. You must also have the cables and device driver software.

Review Questions

Answer the following questions to check your understanding of the lesson material.

1. What is the function of an input device?

2. What does GIGO stand for?

3. What does a device driver do?

4. List four different types of computer keyboard keys.

5. Explain what a mouse is used for.

6. Explain the difference between a drawing pad and a pen-based handwriting pad.

7. List four different types of visual input devices and explain what kind of input each device can recognize.

8. The two different types of image scanners are the _____ and the _____.

9. Explain five different problems involved in voice recognition.

10. What three questions should you ask when purchasing an input device?

3

The System and Central Processing Units

Learning Objectives

- Describe how data is represented in the digital format.

- Define the concepts of bits and bytes.

- Identify the system unit and its components.

- Describe the motherboard, RAM, secondary and primary storage.

- State the components of the CPU.

- Define an expansion slot and expansion card.

- Differentiate between the three main data bus systems.

- Show how a parallel and serial port work.

- Outline the meaning of clock speed.

- Identify the basic difference between IBM and Apple computers.

- Describe the differences between Intel's CPU chips.

You have learned how data and information are input into the computer for processing. This lesson will describe what happens to the data after it gets inside the computer and how the processing takes place. The component that actually does the processing is the central processing unit (CPU). The CPU is often referred to as a "computer on a chip" since it is contained on an electronic circuit chip. The CPU is housed in the system unit — a good place for us to begin looking at how the computer processes information.

The System Unit

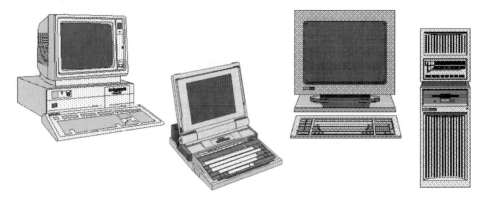

Various types of system units

Personal computers are usually made up of several different components, such as the keyboard, monitor, and *system unit*. Typically, the system unit is a cabinet that houses many electronic components and serves as the main connecting point for other devices of the computer. System units are available in several different styles, including the desktop, tower, and laptop models illustrated above. While the cases are different, as seen below, each system unit contains many of the same components that enable the computer to process information.

The system unit in the desktop model computer furnishes the base for the monitor; while in the tower configuration, the system unit stands on its side and is often placed on the floor next to a desk. The main advantage of the tower configuration is that less desk space is used by the computer. Both the desktop and tower system unit designs typically allow you to add many features to the computer by just plugging in the new device.

The laptop computer combines most components into one small case, saving space and weight. Because of its small size, it is usually more difficult to add new features to a laptop than a desktop or tower model computer.

The Motherboard

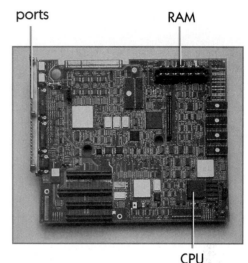

ports   RAM

CPU

2.

One of the main components in the system unit cabinet is a large, printed circuit board which is called the *motherboard*. The motherboard provides connections to all of the components of the computer, including the keyboard, disk drives, monitor, and other peripheral devices. In addition, the motherboard contains the special electronic chip called the *central processing unit* (CPU). Computer manufacturers plug the CPU chip into a special socket on the motherboard. In some computers, called *upgradable systems*, it is possible to unplug the existing CPU chip and replace it with a more powerful chip as they are developed in the future.

The motherboard also provides various expansion sockets or *ports* that allow you to plug in special devices such as a mouse or printer and other special sockets where additional memory or primary storage can be added.

The Central Processing Unit

The central processing unit (CPU) is the main component of the computer and performs all the processing of information. The CPU consists of a small electronic chip called a *microprocessor*. This microprocessor contains many thousands of miniature electronic components on a piece of silicon smaller than a postage stamp.

Relative size of
a CPU chip

3.

The CPU is made up of two components: the *control unit* and the *arithmetic logic unit* (ALU). The control unit is in charge of all the operations in the computer while the ALU performs all arithmetic and logical comparison operations. Arithmetic operations include the usual addition, subtraction, multiplication, and division of numbers. The logical comparison operation compares numbers to see if they are equal or if one is larger or smaller than another. Although the functions performed by the ALU may seem simple, they form the heart of the computer's immense processing power.

How The CPU Works With Data

The computer is a very powerful machine that can perform many calculations per second through the use of electronic circuits. Surprisingly, the computer can do all of its functions by simply detecting if electricity is on or off in a given circuit position. This concept is just like a light switch in your home, in that the switch can be on or off. Instead of light switches, computers use tiny electronic switches that can

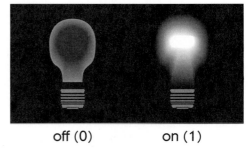

off (0)   on (1)

also be turned on or off. By recognizing if these switches are in the on or off position, the computer can associate data with the switch positions. If only one switch were available on the computer, a 1 could be represented when the switch was on. Conversely, when the switch was off, a zero would be represented.

Bits and Bytes

This on-off (or 1, 0) pattern is the basis for data representation in the computer. Because only 1's and 0's are used, this is said to be a *binary* representation of data. Since each switch or binary position can take on only one of two values (0 and 1), computers must use several binary positions to store one character (a letter of the alphabet, symbol, or number) of information. Most personal computers use eight binary positions to represent one character of data.

These binary positions are called *binary digits* in the computer world; you will usually see this shortened to the term *bit*. Therefore, one bit in the computer refers to one binary digit or a 1 or 0.

Eight bits can then be grouped together to represent a character; in computer terminology, one character is called a *byte*. For example, to represent the word DATA in the computer you would need four characters or bytes. If each byte requires eight bits, a total of 32 bits would be used inside the computer to represent the word DATA.

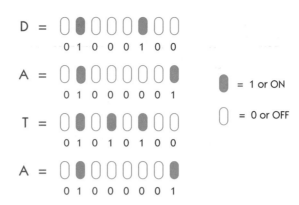

D = ◯ ⬛ ◯ ◯ ◯ ◯ ⬛ ◯ ◯
　　0 1 0 0 0 1 0 0

A = ◯ ⬛ ◯ ◯ ◯ ◯ ◯ ⬛
　　0 1 0 0 0 0 0 1

⬛ = 1 or ON

◯ = 0 or OFF

T = ◯ ⬛ ◯ ⬛ ◯ ⬛ ◯ ◯
　　0 1 0 1 0 1 0 0

A = ◯ ⬛ ◯ ◯ ◯ ◯ ◯ ⬛
　　0 1 0 0 0 0 0 1

The word DATA in ASCII binary representation

The ASCII and EBCDIC Code Standards

To eliminate confusion, standards for binary representation have been set so that each pattern of bits means the same thing from computer to computer. The most common standard for microcomputers is the American Standard Code for Information Interchange (abbreviated as ASCII). Without this standard, it would be very difficult to exchange information between different computers.

Large mainframe computers use a different code called Extended Binary Coded Decimal Interchange Code (EBCDIC) which was developed by the IBM Corporation. While the patterns of bits differ somewhat from the ASCII code, the concept of using a series of bits to represent a character is the same.

CPU Clock Speeds

8. The speed with which the computer can operate is directly related to the *clock speed* of the CPU. The clock speed determines how fast the CPU chip can perform a given calculation and is measured in megahertz (MHz) or one million electronic cycles per second. The faster the computer's clock speed, the more processing it can do in one second and the more powerful the computer is. Early computers had clock speeds of some 4 to 6 MHz while newer systems have reached 66 MHz. Most experts expect clock speeds of 100 MHz in the very near future.

Fast clock speeds are important when your work includes calculating long columns of numbers in a spreadsheet or doing intensive graphics work such as computer-assisted design. It usually makes sense to invest in the fastest clock speed that your budget allows.

Different Types of CPUs

The computer clock speed is an important determinant of a computer's power, but an even more critical factor is the computer's CPU chip type. When looking for a new computer, first consider which CPU chip you will need; then look at the other factors. This means that a more powerful CPU chip running at 20 MHz would be preferred to a less powerful CPU running at 25 MHz.

Personal computer CPUs are constantly being upgraded to provide more power and speed to the user. Surprisingly, even with these dramatic improvements, the cost of computers continues to decline. Some of the most exciting changes have been found in the advances of the CPUs themselves. Many of these advances have been developed by the Intel Corporation which has designed and built most of the CPU chips in today's personal computers. Non-IBM computers that also use the Intel CPU are compatible with the IBM machine and now are called IBM compatible computers or IBM clones.

An IBM PS/2 and an
IBM-compatible

CPU Word Size

One of the most important measures of the processing ability of a CPU chip is its *word size*. The word size of the CPU represents the number of bits that the CPU can process at one time. If a CPU chip processed 8 bits (or one byte) at a time, it would have a word size of 8 bits. Similarly, a CPU with a word size of 16 bits could process twice as much information as the 8-bit machine. Often, machines are classified by the word size and called 8-bit, 16-bit or 32-bit machines. It is important to realize that a computer with a 32-bit CPU chip will process four times as much information as the 8-bit computer for each processor cycle. When this large word size is coupled with fast clock speeds, it is possible to have a very high performance computer.

Storage Concepts

The computer can process considerable amounts of information quickly and

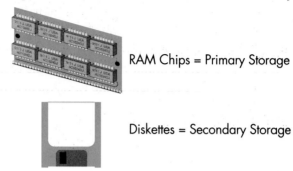

RAM Chips = Primary Storage

Diskettes = Secondary Storage

accurately, but before processing can occur, the computer must be able to access the information in the binary form. To provide this access, the computer uses *storage* which is broken down into two types: *primary* and *secondary* storage.

Primary Storage

Primary storage, also called *memory*, provides the CPU with a temporary space in which information can be manipulated: this space consists of special memory circuit chips that are installed on the motherboard. The most common form of primary storage or memory is *random access memory* (called RAM).

Random access memory or RAM, is used by the computer to store information, programs, or other data that will be used by the CPU for processing. The CPU can both read and write on RAM which then forms a temporary workspace for the computer.

The capacity of a computer's RAM is measured in bytes or characters. Today's computers have thousands to millions of bytes of RAM available. To make it easy to talk about RAM amounts, the terms "K" (an approximation for one thousand), "mega" (one million), and "giga" (one billion) are used. For example, a computer with 640K bytes of RAM would have about 640,000 bytes of RAM. Similarly, a machine with 8 megabytes of RAM would have about 8 million bytes available. Normally, more powerful computers will be equipped with more RAM than smaller machines. Random access memory, since it uses electronic circuit chips to store data, operates fast but is expensive when compared to secondary storage.

Random Access Memory Is Volatile

An important point to remember when using the computer is that data stored in RAM will be lost when the power to the computer is turned off. This is because RAM is *volatile* and is erased when electrical power is removed. For this reason, you should save information to a secondary storage device like a diskette before you turn off the computer. This also means that if you are working on your computer and there is a power failure, *everything that you have done since you last saved to secondary storage will be lost.* For this reason, it is a good practice to save your work frequently to the secondary storage system on your computer.

Secondary Storage

Secondary storage is used to provide a permanent storage location for informa-

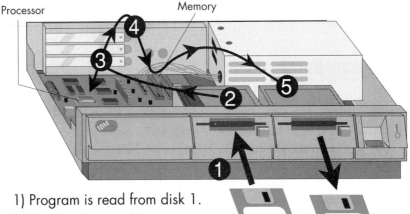

1) Program is read from disk 1.
2) Program is stored in memory.
3) Program instructions are executed by processor.
4) Data is input, stored, and processed.
5) Results are output and saved to disk 2.

The processing cycle

tion and is usually found in the form of diskettes or hard disks. Disks store information magnetically and must be rotated mechanically like a long play record before the information on them can be accessed. This means that these secondary storage devices are much slower to operate than RAM; however, unlike RAM, they can store vast amounts of information inexpensively. You will learn more about secondary storage devices in Lesson 5.

To optimize the speed of the computer, yet at the same time to minimize the cost and allow vast amounts of information to be accessible, the computer uses primary and secondary storage as a team. When the CPU needs information from a secondary storage device like a disk, it is first read from the disk into RAM. The CPU will then read the information from RAM, process it, and return the result back to RAM. When the information is saved to disk, it is moved from RAM and returned to the disk.

Special Types of Storage

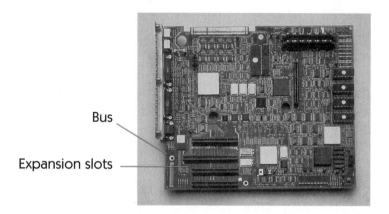

Bus

Expansion slots

There are a few special storage topics of which you need to be aware. First, most computers are equipped with special _read only memory_ or ROM. This memory cannot be written to like RAM and cannot be erased when the power is turned off. Therefore, it is usually used by the computer manufacturer to store special instructions for the computer's use such as controlling the monitor or keyboard.

Another type of storage is _cache memory_. This is a special kind of RAM that serves as a buffer between slower secondary storage and the very fast RAM. The cache tries to predict what information the CPU will need next and then loads it from the disk into the cache memory. When the CPU needs the information, it is immediately available in the cache memory. In this way, the cache memory reduces the CPU waiting time that would occur while the disk is searched for needed information. Cache memory is usually found on the personal computers with larger cache sizes (in terms of "K") usually indicating faster computers.

The Data Bus

Since the CPU does all the processing in the personal computer, connections must be provided so that information can be input and output to other devices. To provide this connection, the personal computer is equipped with a data bus which serves as an electronic highway on the motherboard between the CPU and other components.

The computer data bus also has places to plug in other devices, both under the system unit cover and at the back of the computer. This expansion ability allows you to add options to the computer easily without having to know anything about electronics. The actual receptacles that are used to provide this expansion are called *expansion slots*.

Expansion Slots

If you were to take the cover of the system unit off, you would notice that there are several special receptacles located on the motherboard. These sockets are the expansion slots and allow you to plug in special electronic circuit boards that perform additional processing functions. These plug-in boards are called *expansion cards* or *add-on cards*, and can provide you with extra RAM, fax capabilities, telephone connections, and much more. For example, if you use a color monitor with your computer, you will also usually need to add an expansion card inside the computer to which the monitor will attach. By using expansion cards and slots to add features to the computer, it is easier to make the computer do exactly what you need it to do. This ability to enhance your personal computer by simply plugging in an expansion card contributes greatly to the computer's flexibility and popularity.

Available Data Bus Systems

There are three different data bus systems available and choosing the best one for your needs is an important decision to make when selecting a computer. One big difference in the available bus systems is the bus capacity. Bus capacity is analogous to traffic on a highway. If one highway has four lanes and another has eight lanes available, it is easy to see that the eight-lane road will be able to carry much more traffic. Data bus systems are similar, with one bus carrying 16 bits of data at a time and the other two having a 32-bit capacity. This means that the larger bus can move twice as much information at the same time between the CPU, RAM, disk drives, and other computer devices. As a result, the larger 32-bit bus systems offer considerably higher performance potential.

ISA	16 bits
EISA	32 bits
MCA	32 bits

The most popular data bus is called ①
the Industry Standard Architecture (ISA for short) and is more than sufficient for most personal use. This data bus is capable of moving 16 bits (or two bytes) of data at a time and has many different expansion cards available for it. The main attraction of this data bus system is its low cost and widespread acceptance.

②

The Enhanced Industry Standard Architecture (EISA) bus is an extension of the ISA bus and can move 32 bits of data at a time. This gives the EISA bus a significant performance advantage over the ISA bus. Further, the EISA bus has been designed so that the original ISA expansion cards can be used. This means it is compatible with many older computers. The EISA costs significantly more than the ISA systems and is best suited to high performance machines.

③

The final bus system called Micro Channel Architecture (MCA), was developed by the IBM Corporation and can handle 32 bits of data at a time. While MCA is a very capable system, it is not compatible with either ISA or EISA expansion cards.This means you could not exchange expansion cards between the MCA bus computers and other computers. This powerful bus system is popular in firms that have many IBM systems installed.

Which Bus Should I Choose?

Let's consider the highway analogy again to answer this question. Certainly the eight-lane highway has the potential to carry more traffic than the four-lane highway. However, if the traffic flow is light, either highway will be able to handle the load. Only when the traffic builds to a point that the four lane road is congested will the eight lane road offer an improvement. Until that point, the eight-lane road does little to help traffic capacity, and it will cost much more.

Bus systems can be thought of in the same light. The ISA bus will work very well for almost all personal computer use simply because few users will be able to generate enough traffic to cause congestion on the bus. For business or network systems, this will be a different story, and the larger, more expensive EISA or MCA systems will be preferred.

Parallel and Serial Ports

A parallel port   A serial port

(#'s in order veetically in a
column)

(#'s in a series horizontally)

When you look at the back of the system unit, you will see several receptacles which are called *ports*. These ports allow you to connect a number of external devices to the computer, including printers, modems, a mouse, and many other items. You will also notice that there are two different kinds of ports: one is a *parallel port* and the other is a *serial port*. Each port works in a different way, and it is important to know the general characteristics of each one.

Parallel Ports

Parallel ports work by sending several bits at a time to the device, usually a printer, that is plugged into the port. In this way, the port can transmit an entire byte or character (eight bits) at a time. This provides very fast information transfer, but the connected device needs to be located close (within 20 feet) of the computer. The most common use of the parallel port is to connect a printer to the computer.

Serial Ports

The serial port transmits data to a connected device one bit at a time. To send one byte (eight bits), it must send each bit individually. This means that the serial port will normally operate slower than the parallel port where eight bits can be sent at once. Serial ports are commonly used to connect a mouse or modem to the computer.

IBM-Compatible Central Processing Unit Computers

IBM PC and
8088 chip

One of the earliest personal computers to use the Intel CPU was the original IBM Personal Computer or PC which was sold in the early 1980's. This computer used the Intel 8088 CPU chip which provided for 16-bit processing. This meant that the CPU could handle the processing of two bytes or characters at a time. Unfortunately, even though the CPU could work with 16 bits of information, the data bus could only work with 8 bits at a time which is too slow for many new program requirements. Its clock speed was 4.77 MHz, and it was the first personal computer to use the now familiar MS DOS operating system. This computer could accommodate a maximum of 640K of RAM which is not enough for many of the newer software programs.

The IBM-AT and 80286 chip

The next step up in the Intel/IBM compatible market is represented by computers built on the Intel 80286 CPU. This is an advanced 16 bit processor and is capable of using large amounts of RAM. This computer uses the ISA data bus and is probably the minimum computer that most users should consider purchasing. Clock speeds of the '286 machines range from 16 to 25 MHz.

The current state-of-the-art computers are based on the Intel 80386 and 80486 CPU chips. The 80386 CPU is available in two different models: the '386 SX and the '386 DX. The 80386 SX model has a 32-bit word size but is fitted to a 16-bit bus system. The more powerful 80386 DX chip uses a full 32-bit bus for data transfer. Unless your needs are limited to relatively simple requirements, you would be well advised to consider the 80386 DX model.

The 80486 is also available in two models called the SX and DX; however, the difference between them is not the same as in the '386 chip line. The 80486 DX is equipped with special circuitry that allows it to compute special mathematical routines very rapidly. This built-in *math coprocessor* will be a big help in calculating rows of numbers, simulation models, or in many graphic design programs. The SX model of the '486 is exactly the same as the DX except that it does not offer the built in math coprocessor. Both the SX and the DX models work with a 32-bit word size and offer a full 32-bit bus structure. Clock speeds are available from 25 to 66 MHz.

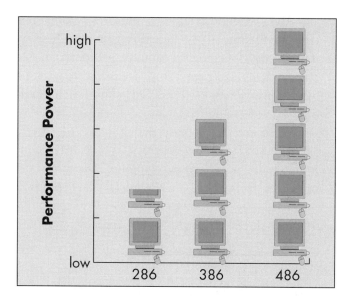

Given recent declines in the prices of these computers, it makes sense to consider the purchase of a '386 DX or '486 SX or DX rather than a much less powerful '286 system. The larger computer will provide reasonable growth options and will retain its value much longer than the almost obsolete 80286 based machine. Further, new 80486 based machines are built with upgradable CPU chips that can be replaced with new CPU models as they become available.

Apple Personal Computers

The Apple
Macintoshes

The Apple Macintosh family of personal computers represents the leading alternative to the Intel/IBM compatible systems. These systems use a CPU chip series that was developed by the Motorola Corporation. Motorola numbers their CPU chips much like the Intel chips are numbered, with higher number chips being more powerful. All Motorola CPU chips accommodate a 32-bit word size and offer extremely powerful computing capability.

The 68020 CPU is now the entry CPU in the Macintosh computer line and is found in the Macintosh LC computer. The more powerful 68030 chip found in upper-end LC models, the Macintosh Classic/30 and the Macintosh Si, offers performance roughly equal to the Intel 80486 based IBM compatible computers. The highest performance Motorola processor, the 68040, is found in the multi-user Macintosh Quadra computer.

The Macintosh offers some other unique capabilities in that it was designed to operate in a graphic or picture based environment. This means that tasks involving graphics, such as animation, desktop publishing, and graphic-based presentations are very well suited for the Macintosh. IBM compatible computers can also perform these tasks but not with the same ease of use, although the IBM compatible machines continue to improve in this area.

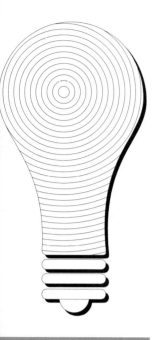

Summary

System Unit Components

- The system unit is the heart of the computer system and contains a main circuit board called the motherboard.

- The central processing unit is an electronic chip that does all the processing in the computer and is located on the motherboard. The CPU can only process information in a binary or digital format.

Data Storage and Memory

- The smallest component of data is called a binary digit, or BIT, with each bit made up of a 1 or 0. Several bits (usually 8) are grouped together to form characters or bytes. These bits and bytes are processed by the CPU and then saved in primary or secondary storage.

- Primary storage (also called <u>random access storage</u>) is <u>volatile</u> and is erased when the computer's power is turned off.

Computer Performance Factors

chip
- The CPU <u>clock speed</u> which determines how fast a given <u>CPU will operate</u>. *chip* Faster clock speeds mean the CPU will be capable of performing more processing during the same period of time.

chips
- CPU's are categorized by the number of bits it can process at one time. This is called the CPU word size and most CPUs now offer a word size of 16 or 32 bits. *chip*

- There are three widely available IBM compatible bus systems, the ISA bus can move 16 bits while the MCS and EISA can both work with 32 bits at a time.

- The Apple Macintosh computer family offers powerful, yet easy to use computers with some important advantages over the more common IBM compatible computers but usually at a higher cost.

CPU = Central Processing Unit = the electronic chip

Review Questions

Answer the following questions to check your understanding of the lesson material.

1. The "computer on a chip" located on the motherboard is called the
   _____.

2. Name four devices that are connected to the motherboard.

3. What does ALU stand for and what does it do?

4. Define a bit and a byte.

5. How are bits combined to represent a byte?

6. What is primary storage?

7. Why is RAM said to be volatile?

8. What does clock speed mean?

9. To install a new color monitor, you will likely need to add a _____
   card into an _____ slot on the motherboard.

10. Name the three common IBM compatible data bus designs. Which is the
    least powerful?

11. What is the difference between a serial and parallel port?

Output Devices

Learning Objectives

■ Explain the function of an output device.

■ Explain the difference between soft copy and hard copy output and output devices.

■ List at least five important characteristics of computer monitors.

■ Explain the function of graphic adapters.

■ Distinguish between four different types of computer video displays.

■ List at least six important characteristics of computer printers.

■ Identify three different common types of printers for microcomputers.

■ Explain the difference between two types of plotters.

■ List three different types of audio output devices.

■ Define the terms CGA, EGA, VGA, SVGA, XGA, pixel, LCD, proportional printing, DPI, dot matrix, and font.

Once the data has been input through the input devices, and processed using the processor and some software program, it is then normally output or stored. In this lesson we will discuss output and output devices. We will discuss storage and storage devices later in Lesson 5.

As with input devices, it is important to remember that you must have *device drivers* for output devices. The drivers are software programs that tell the output devices how to operate. A reference to a device driver may not be made, but you should remember that one is required.

What Is Output?

Output is the third step in the *input-process-output* cycle. In the example we used in Lesson 2, the input was three test scores, processing was the averaging of the three scores, and the output was the average. In most cases, output is the result of calculating, rearranging, reformatting or otherwise manipulating the raw input data. In some cases, the output may be exactly the same as the raw input data. As a reminder, output will be no more accurate than the input that you start with— remember GIGO (garbage-in, garbage-out).

In order to output information you must have some type of output device. These output devices are hardware. There are many different types of output devices, each type having many different variations. We will only discuss some of these in this lesson. For consistency with the lesson on input devices, we will group these output devices into three categories — visual, touch, and sound.

Visual Output Devices

Visual output devices provide output that you can see, but not touch. This type of output is referred to as *soft copy* since you cannot hold it in your hands. Some of the most common devices that fall into this category are monitors, screen projectors, and film recorders.

Monitors

The computer monitor is the most common visual output device. A monitor looks much like a TV, and most monitors have controls to adjust the brightness and the contrast of the screen. The monitor serves as a window which allows you to see what is in the memory of the machine. In some cases, the monitor is the only output device that a micro-computer has.

Most monitors are of the cathode ray tube type. These types of monitors have a coating of phosphorus particles on their screens. To display images on the screen, an electron gun scans the screen hundreds of times per second firing beams at the areas of phosphorus. When the phosphorus is hit by the beam, it is lighted. By hitting different areas on the screen, characters and other images are formed. These lighted areas are called pixels or picture elements.

There are several characteristics of a monitor of which you should be aware. We will discuss some of the more important ones.

Monitor Size

The size of a computer monitor is determined by the diagonal measurement of the screen. Monitor sizes may vary anywhere from five inches to several feet. The most common sizes are 12 and 14 inches. Smaller screens are normally found on laptop and notebook computers. Larger screens are normally used with desktop publishing, page layout, and graphic design systems.

Monochrome Versus Color

The monitor type is also important. There are two different types of monitors — monochrome and color. Monochrome monitors usually display only two colors such as black and white, amber and white, or green and white. Some mono-chrome monitors can display one or two shades of gray as well. These types of monitors are acceptable if most of your work involves text or numbers, but they are not acceptable if you intend to do much art work, graphing, or game playing.

The second type of monitor is a color monitor. These monitors are often called RGB monitors for the three colors that are used (red, green, and blue). Color monitors can display anywhere from 4 up to 32,676 different colors. In order for the color monitors to display the colors, you must also have a color graphics-adapter card installed in your machine. The thing to remember is that a color monitor alone will not give your computer system the ability to display color. You must have both the color monitor and the color graphics adapter card.

Output Devices

59

Currently there are five basic graphic adapter cards. They are:

CGA (color graphics adapter): This is the oldest of the adapter cards. This card provides the minimal number of colors (4) and some limited graphics capability.

EGA (enhanced graphics adapter): This adapter card is still commonly found on microcomputer systems. The card will give you up to 16 different colors.

VGA (video graphics array): This card will provide up to 256 different colors. Most new computer systems use this card as their standard graphics card.

SVGA (super video graphics array): This card is common on the more expensive microcomputer systems. This adapter card can provide up to 256 different colors simultaneously. This card provides the same number of colors as a standard VGA card but it provides higher resolution (covered later).

XGA (extended graphics adapter): This is the newest, most advanced of the graphics adapters. This adapter, with the proper monitor, can display 32,676 different colors simultaneously.

The adapter cards not only give you the ability to display color, they also help determine the clarity of both the graphics and the text on the screen. This clarity is referred to as a monitor's *resolution*, the next characteristic of a monitor.

Resolution

Characters that are displayed on a monitor are created by a set of very small, lighted dots. These lighted dots are referred to as *pixels* which is short for the term *picture element*. A character is created by a set of picture elements, or pixels. When only a few pixels are used to create a character, the character's shape is not as clear as it would be if a large number of pixels were used to create the same character. The number of pixels available on a screen determines a screen's *resolution*.

Low resolution monitors may have a pixel density of 320 X 200 pixels. This is 320 pixels horizontally and 200 pixels vertically. A 320 X 200 pixel density

High resolution character

768 X 1,024 = 786,432

Low resolution character

320 X 320 = 64,000

would provide a total of 64,000 pixels for the entire screen. A high resolution screen may provide a 768 X 1,024 pixel density. This would give you a total of 786,432 pixels for the entire screen. Since you have more points of light in a given area, you would have more points of light to create a given character and the character would be much clearer. Therefore, high resolution screens provide a much clearer and sharper image on the screen.

Graphics adapter cards were discussed earlier with color monitors. The adapter card not only provides the color capability, but it also helps provide the monitor's resolution. For example a CGA adapter card provides a pixel density of 320 X 200 when colors are displayed. A XGA card, with the proper monitor, can provide a pixel density of 768 X 1,024 when only 16 colors are being displayed.

GRAPHIC ADAPTERS

ADAPTER	MAXIMUM NUMBER OF COLORS	MAXIMUM RESOLUTION
CGA	4	320 x 200 = 64,000 pixels
EGA	16	640 x 350 = 224,000 pixels
VGA	16	640 x 480 = 307,200 pixels
SVGS	256	800 x 600 = 480,000 pixels
XGA	32,676	1024 x 768 = 786,432 pixels

The resolution possible for a particular system depends upon both the monitor and the adapter card. The highest resolution possible will be the resolution of the lowest of the two. For example, if the monitor supports a maximum resolution of 640 X 480 but your adapter card is a SVGA card that supports 800 X 600 resolution, your maximum resolution will be that of the monitor, 640 X 480.

Flat Screen Displays

The monitors discussed above have a large picture tube in them. This picture tube has a _yoke_, like a normal TV, which forces the monitor to have a deep screen. They also consume a considerable amount of energy. Because of their size, weight, and power consumption, these larger monitors are unsuitable for many applications such as laptop and notebook computers. To solve this problem, there have been several flat screen displays developed. Flat screen displays do not have the high resolution of standard monitors but are much smaller, lighter, and more portable. They also consume less energy which makes them more suitable for an application where battery power is used.

2.

Liquid Crystal Displays (LCD)

A liquid crystal display

The most common flat screen display is the liquid crystal. This technology uses two thin layers of glass with a liquid chemical trapped between them. A chemical reaction turns the chemical dark when electricity is passed through thin wires in the display. These darkened chemicals block the light that forms the image of a character.

The primary advantages of LCDs are their light weight and low energy consumption. Their primary disadvantage is that they require light from the environment. This light requirement makes them difficult to read in areas where little light is present. LCDs are available today that support VGA standards and display up to 256 colors. As the resolution and color capability of these displays improve and the price decreases, you may see the LCD replace the standard monitor for desktop computers.

3.

Electroluminescent Display

Electroluminescent displays are another type of flat screen display. This technology uses a grid of small wires embedded in a specially treated material that glows in response to electricity. Each point where two wires cross forms a pixel.

The biggest drawback to this technology is that it currently does not have the ability to display color. If color can be developed for this technology, it could match or surpass the capabilities of the cathode ray technology.

MONITOR CONSUMER TIPS

- **Size:** Diagonal measurement of the display area of the screen.

- **Monochrome or Color:** Monochrome is two colors only. Color can display anywhere from 4 to 32,676 different colors.

- **Resolution:** Number of pixels available on the screen. Low resolution: 320 X 200, High Resolution: 768 X 1,024

- **Graphics Adapter:** CGA, EGA, VGA, SVGA, XGA

- **Display Technology:** cathode ray tube (CRT), liquid crystal display (LCD), or electroluminescent display

4. ## Screen Image Projectors

Screen image projectors are devices that are used to display the computer's images on a wide projection screen. The screen image projector is placed on top of an overhead projector and is connected to an output *port* on the microcomputer. The image projector captures the output from the computer and the overhead projects the image on the wide screen.

These devices are excellent for presentations and demonstrations. You can use these devices to show large groups of people exactly what is occurring on the computer monitor. The presentation is *live*, as the computer generates its output. If you need to make changes to your presentation material, you could conceivably make them as you are giving your presentation.

advantage *✗*

5. ## Film Recorders

Film recorders send their output directly to a 35 mm film strip. These devices are excellent for creating presentations. Using these devices, you can create a presentation on your computer, create a film strip of the presentation, then use the film strip to make your presentation.

The advantage of film recorders is that you do not need the computer when you make the presentation; all you need is a 35 mm projector and a projection screen.

The disadvantage of the film recorder (over a screen image projector) is that if you need to change the images in your presentation, you would need to create a new film strip. If you were using a screen image projector, you could make the changes to the presentation anytime.

Output You Can Touch

Many times you want output that you can touch. For example, you may need to make copies of a report and distribute these copies to members of a team, or you may simply want to take the output with you without taking your computer and monitor. Output that you can touch is referred to as *hard copy* output.

The most common output devices that produce output you can touch are printers. There are hundreds of different makes, models, and styles of printers. Each type of printer has its advantages and disadvantages. We will first discuss some of the important characteristics of printers, then we will discuss some of the types of printers.

Characteristics of Printers

The two most important characteristics of a printer are its speed and quality. Other important characteristics include the way it prints, a character at a time versus a page at a time, whether it uses an impact or non-impact technology, and whether characters and spaces are proportional or fixed in size.

1. **Speed:** A printer's speed is measured by the number of characters printed per second (*CPS*), or by the number of pages printed per minute (*PPM*) depending upon the technique used by the printer. Typical printer speeds for character printers are 40 to 260 CPS, depending upon the printer and the quality of the print. Page printer speeds range from 4 to 25 PPM.

2. **Quality:** Print quality means how clear and sharp the characters appear when they are printed. Most printers form their characters using a pattern of small dots, much the same as a monitor uses *pixels* to form images. The number of possible dots per inch, referred to as *DPI*, determines a printer's print quality or resolution. For computer printers there are four print modes or print qualities.

   Draft: This mode uses the minimum number of dots per inch. The characters are not very clear or sharp but are normally printed at the maximum speed for the printer. Use this mode when you need a hard copy for proof-reading.

NLQ (Near Letter Quality): This mode provides a much clearer and sharper character than draft quality because it uses more dots per inch, but it normally prints slower. Most, but not all, printers support the NLQ mode.

LQ (Letter Quality): Letter quality mode, as the name implies, is suitable for producing professional correspondence. This mode provides a clear crisp image of the characters and looks as though it were produced on a high quality typewriter.

NTQ (Near Typeset Quality): This mode is suitable for published material such as books and magazines. The images are very clear and crisp and this mode normally requires a print resolution of 300 DPI or better.

3. **Character vs. page printing**: Some printers print only one character at a time, much like a typewriter. These printers have a *print head* that moves across the paper printing characters as it moves. Other printers print an entire page at one time, much like a copier. Page printers are normally much faster than character printers.

4. **Impact vs. non-impact:** Many printers use a technology that uses impact to form the character's image. When impact technology is used, some device will strike a *hammer* that strikes a printer ribbon, which strikes the paper and leaves the image. These types of printers are usually noisy and unsuitable in environments where a low noise level is necessary. One advantage of impact printers is that you can use multi-part paper and make carbon copies. Other printers use a technology that does not cause impact on the paper. These types of printers are good when low noise levels are required. Their primary disadvantage is that they cannot make carbon copies.

5. **Proportional printing:** Many printers use the same amount of space to form the letter *I* or a blank space as they do to form the letter *M.* This can leave large gaps between words when margins are justified; this can make reading of the text more difficult. These types of printers are referred to as non-proportional printers. Other printers use a varying amount of space to form characters, depending upon the width of the character. These printers are proportional printers. Proportional printers also use less space for blank spaces. Proportional printers create a much more professional document than non-proportional (monospace) printers and are required for near typeset quality.

Dot Matrix Printers

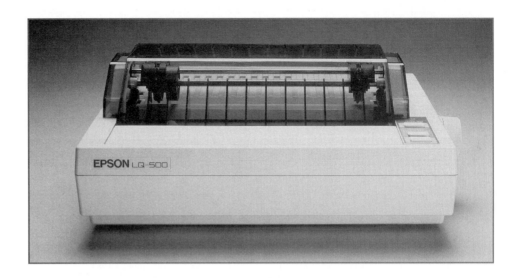

A dot matrix
printer

Dot matrix printers use an impact technology and normally print only one character at a time. This type of printer has a print head that is composed of a column of small *pins*. To form a character, a small hammer strikes certain pins that in turn strike an inked ribbon. The ink on the ribbon leaves part of the character's image. The print head then moves forward (about 1/1000 of an inch), and other pins are struck to form more of the character. In order to form a character, it takes several head movements and hammer strikes. The print head moves across the page, forming part of a character each time it moves.

Much of the print quality for dot matrix printers is determined by the number of pins on the print head. The more pins you have, the more dots per inch you can get; therefore, the higher the quality of the print. Printers with more pins also normally print faster. Nine, eighteen, and twenty-four pin print heads are common.

Most dot matrix printers can print in draft and NLQ mode. When dot matrix printers print in NLQ mode, they actually print the character twice, changing the location of the print head by a fraction of an inch each time they print. This is the reason why printing in NLQ mode is slower than printing in draft mode. Some dot matrix printer manufactures advertise a letter quality mode, but whether it is truly letter quality is still debatable. Many dot matrix printers can also output proportional printing.

Dot matrix printers can print graphs and pictures, but these normally print very slowly, depending upon the resolution of the graph or picture. You can also print color with many dot matrix printers. When color is used on dot matrix printers, you use a multicolor printer ribbon and you need a printer *driver* that can take advantage of the color capability. Because of the colors available on the ribbon, the number of colors is limited. Not all dot matrix printers support color printing.

Dot matrix printers are common types of printers for personal microcomputer systems because of their low cost. Dot matrix printers sell for between $100 to $1000 with good printers averaging about $500. They are impact printers so they are not good for areas where noise level is important, for example, libraries or professional offices. Until recently, dot matrix output was not considered acceptable for professional correspondence. Today, most people accept this type of output in professional letters when it is printed in near letter quality or letter quality mode.

2. Inkjet Printers

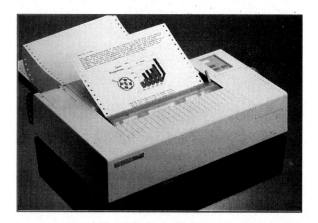

An inkjet printer

Inkjet printers are another type of character printer, but they are non-impact printers. These types of printers use ink wells rather than inked ribbons. To print a character or image, the print head sprays droplets of ink onto the paper. Since the ink is sprayed, it has a chance to flow together and give a better print quality (letter quality) than most dot matrix printers. A special quick drying ink must be used to keep the ink from running and smearing too much.

Most inkjet printers can also produce color. Some printers use a single cartridge that contains all the colors. When one color runs out, you must replace the entire cartridge, wasting a great deal of ink for the seldomly used colors. Other printers use different cartridges for each color. These printers allow you to replace one color at a time, and this ends up being cheaper when most of your work is predominately one color. The cheaper inkjet printers have a limited number of colors available but can mix the ink sprays to provide shades of other colors. Some of the more expensive color printers can print as many as 250,000 different colors.

Most inkjet printers are considered letter quality (LQ) printers and print at between 200 and 280 dots per inch. They are more expensive than dot matrix printers, starting at around $400 and running up to $4,000. Their primary advantage, along with their quality, is their noise level. Since they are non-impact printers, they are fairly quiet. Their disadvantage is that since they are non-impact, they cannot make carbon copies.

3.
Laser Printers

A laser printer

Laser printers are considered page printers. They print an entire page at a time. The technology of these printers is similar to that of copiers. A laser beam is directed at a light-sensitive printing drum. The laser beam forms an image of dots on the printing drum. This drum then places electrostatic charges on the paper. Next, a toner is deposited on the paper in the charged areas. The toner adhering to the charged areas of the paper forms the printed image.

The quality of laser printers is considered NTQ, near typeset quality. Most smaller laser printers print at 300 DPI, but some of the more expensive ones print at up to 600 or even 1200 DPI. Since they print a page at a time, their speed is measured in pages per minute (PPM). Typical speeds for desktop laser printers range from 5 to 15 PPM. Larger laser printers can print up to 50 PPM. Laser printers are non-impact printers so they are quiet, but they cannot produce carbon copies. The inability to produce a carbon copy however, is not considered a major disadvantage because of the printer's speed, especially when considering the higher print quality. If you need carbon copies, simply print multiple original copies.

Laser printers cost from around $800 up to over $10,000 for desktop laser printers. Larger 600 DPI laser printers that print 25 pages per minute cost between $10,000 and $20,000. Most laser printers print only black characters. You can buy color laser printers, but their costs are in the upper end of the price range, in the $8,000 to $10,000 price range for desktop laser printers.

Most laser printers support a larger variety of *fonts* and *font sizes*. A font is the shape or type of a character. When producing published material, you often want to use different character shapes for things such as headings, picture captions, notes, or other things you want to stand out from the body of the document.

Also you often want to use different font sizes. A font's size is measured in *points*. A point is 1/72 of an inch. By combining different fonts and font sizes, you can create outstanding documents, advertisements, brochures, and many other kinds of printed material. Many laser printers have built-in fonts. This means certain font styles and sizes come as part of the printer hardware. Other fonts are *downloadable* fonts. These fonts are software. The advantage of built-in fonts is that they print faster. The advantage of downloadable fonts is that you can add more fonts whenever you want to. Most dot matrix and inkjet printers can also print different fonts and font sizes, but the number of fonts and font sizes are very limited, usually three or four.

EXAMPLE OF FONTS AND FONT SIZES

---

8 point Chancery

12 point Times Roman

15 point Avant Garde

20 point Bodoni Poster

Laser printers also produce excellent graphics. One reason is because of their 300 DPI printing density. Another reason is because of their ability to print *postscript images*.

Laser printers are typically used where very high quality hard-copy output is required. Common uses are in professional offices, like lawyers' offices, and in desktop publishing applications (discussed in Lesson 8). As the cost of laser printers continues to come down, you will probably find them in more and more environments.

There are many other types of printers. Some of the printers use mechanical devices for printing, such as a daisy wheel, or print ball. Other printers print a line of text at one time, like chain and drum printers. Even others use a thermal

---

printing technology that uses heat transfer to form images on specially coated paper. Although these types of printers are available, the dot matrix, inkjet, and laser printers are the predominate printers for microcomputer systems.

PRINTER CONSUMER TIPS

Measure of the number of characters printed per minute (CPM) or the number of pages printed per minute (PPM).

- **Quality:** Measured in dots per inch (DPI). Modes are Draft, near letter quality (NLQ), letter quality (LQ), and near typeset quality (NTQ).

- **Character or Page Printing:** Is text printed one character at a time or is it printed one page at a time?

- **Impact or Non-Impact:** Does the printing mechanism make contact with the paper or is another imaging technique used?

- **Proportional Printing:** Do all characters and spaces require the same amount of space horizontally or do narrow characters use less space?

- **Printing Technology:** Dot Matrix, Inkjet, or Laser.

Pen Plotters

Pen plotters are used exclusively for graphic output. These devices use a set of colored pens to draw or *plot* lines on paper output. There are two basic types of pen plotters — flatbed plotters and drum plotters.

A flatbed plotter uses the same approach as the child's *Etch-a-sketch*. A piece of drawing paper is placed on a flat surface called the bed of the plotter. The drawing pens are fixed to the plotter by two wires, one that moves the pen horizontally and one that moves the pen vertically. To draw lines vertically, the vertical wire drags the pen. To draw lines horizontally, the horizontal wire drags the pen. To draw curves, both wires drag the pen a fraction of an inch vertically then a fraction of an inch horizontally.

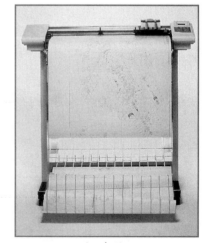

A plotter

A drum plotter uses the same principle as the flatbed plotter except that the paper also moves on a drum plotter. A piece of drawing paper is attached to a drum cylinder. The drawing pen only has a horizontal wire. To draw horizontal lines the wire drags the pen across the paper. To draw vertical lines, the drum is rolled which drags the paper beneath the pen. To draw curves, both the drum and the pen are moved.

Plotters are used by engineers, drafting personnel, map makers, architects, and other professionals that require precise detail in their graphic output. Plotters are often used to keep records of measurements on scientific and industrial devices such as temperature, wind velocity, water levels, and volume of output.

Output You Can Hear

Another type of output devices produce output that you can hear. These devices take the processed data and convert it to sound waves.

Speakers

All speakers take electronic signals and convert them into sound. Since all processing and data stored in a computer consist of electronic signals, all data can be played back through a speaker. In most cases, the sound will appear to be more noise than audible sound, but this variation is because of the data being used to produce the sound.

Today all computers have an internal speaker. The speaker is usually small and simple. It is the speaker that gives you the beeps as you complete tasks or make errors. Using a programming language, you can have your computer play music using this small, simple internal speaker.

You can also connect larger speakers to computer systems. Using the larger speakers, an optical laser disk player (discussed in Lesson 5), and the proper software, you can turn your computer into a high quality stereo with concert-hall sound.

> ### TRY THIS
> Place a small portable radio on top of your system cabinet. Run a program that performs many processing tasks. If you turn on the radio and turn the right frequency, you can hear the processor working through the radio's speaker.

Music Synthesizers

Music synthesizers were discussed in Lesson 2 of the hardware section as input devices. Music synthesizers are also output devices. These devices can take data that has been entered through almost any other device and output that data as sound. Using certain software programs, you can compose the music by typing the notes or scores for the music. Then, using a music synthesizer and speakers, you can have the composed music played for you. Most synthesizers can simulate different instruments with the same notes. These devices can allow you to be your own composer, instrumentalist, and conductor. You would then truly be a one-person band.

Voice Synthesizers

Voice synthesizers promise to be the most exciting and beneficial audio output devices available. Although speech synthesis is fairly crude today, much research and development effort is being placed in this area.

Many of the voice response systems today simply store a pre-recorded voice. When certain voice output is needed, the computer system searches for the correct recording and plays it back.

Voice synthesizers do much more than this. They take stored words and generate their own speech sounds. The current technology uses one of two approaches — *speech coding* or *speech synthesis*.

Speech coding is the simpler of the two approaches. Using this technique, each speech sound is recorded and coded. These coded sounds are then stored and used as building blocks to create the required speech. To generate speech from stored words, each word is broken down into its sound components. The code for each sound component is then determined, and the speech is generated by matching sound codes and playing back the prerecorded speech sounds.

Speech synthesis relies on a set of basic speech sounds generated electronically, without the help of pre-recorded sounds. This technique uses combinations of vowels and consonants to generate sound. Most of the development in voice output is being placed in this speech synthesis area.

The application for speech synthesis is unlimited. For example, imagine a character reader being used as an input device with a speech synthesizer being used as an output device. This combination could allow a blind person to *read*. Also consider the applications possible in language translation. Spanish or some other language could be input and English could be output as speech.

Connecting Output Devices

As with input devices, output devices must be connected to the system unit. Output devices are normally connected to a serial or parallel *port* on the back of the system cabinet. Today's machines will normally have two serial ports and one parallel port. If the built-in ports are being used by another device, you may need to install an expansion board or add-on card to get additional ports. Refer to Lesson 3 of this course for more information about serial and parallel ports.

You must remember that the output devices will require *device drivers*. Most computer programs will provide device drivers for the commonly known printers and plotters. Some of the specialized output devices, like voice synthesizers, will probably provide the device driver with the devices. These device drivers are necessary for the processor and the output device to work together.

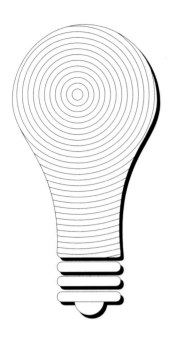

Summary

- Output devices can be grouped into three different categories — devices that produce output you can see, devices that produce output you can touch, and devices that produce output you can hear.

- A monitor is the most common output device that produces output you can only see. This type of output is called soft copy output.

- The important characteristics of a monitor are its size, type (monochrome or color), its resolution, and its display technology. Color and resolution are determined by the adapter card that controls the monitor. The most common display technology for monitors is the cathode ray tube. Flat displays may use the liquid crystal, or electroluminescent display technology.

- Printers produce output you can touch. This type of output is called hard copy. Important characteristics of printers are speed and quality.

- A common printing technology for small printers is the dot matrix technology. Inkjet technology provides a better quality, but is a little more expensive. Laser printers are the most expensive and provide the highest quality. Laser printers also provide more fonts and font sizes.

- The third category of output devices produce output you can hear. Speakers are the simplest device. Music synthesizers allow you to write music scores on the keyboard and play them back through the computer. Speech synthesizers take the electronically coded data and translate it into speech sounds.

- All the output devices need to be connected to either a serial or parallel port. Output devices must also have a software driver to aid in the translation of the data they are outputting.

Review Questions

Answer the following questions to check your understanding of the lesson material.

1. What is the function of an output device?

2. What is the difference between hard copy output and soft copy output? List several devices that produce each type of output.

3. Give five characteristics of a computer monitor.

4. Different graphics-adapters improve two characteristics of soft copy output. What are these two characteristics?

5. How does the technology of a cathode ray tube monitor differ from the technology of a flat screen display?

6. Flat screen displays use _____, _____, or _____ technology to display data.

7. The quality of printed material is determined by the number of _____ used to print the characters.

8. Which printing mode provides the highest quality print — draft, NLQ, LQ, or NTQ?

9. List the three types of microcomputer printers and explain how each type produces its output.

10. List six considerations for buying a computer printer.

11. How does a flatbed plotter differ from a drum plotter?

12. Explain the difference between speech coding and speech synthesis.

Data and Storage Devices

Learning Objectives

- Identify the basic building blocks of data.

- Explain the differences between magnetic storage devices and optical storage devices.

- Distinguish between and list the characteristics of two types of diskettes and diskette drives.

- List the advantages of a hard drive.

- List the advantages and disadvantages of magnetic tape storage media.

- Identify and list advantages and disadvantages of optical storage devices.

- Explain the function of backup.

- Define the terms data density, BPI, CD-ROM, formatting, tracks, sector, and WORM.

S o far, we have discussed three of the principal components of computer systems — input, processing, and output. The next component is storage.

Once data is input it needs to be stored. Remember that the internal memory of the computer, RAM, is limited. RAM is also volatile. This means that the contents of RAM are lost when the power is turned off. Because of the limited memory size and the volatility of RAM, data must be stored using another media if you want to keep it available for an extended period of time. This lesson will cover devices and techniques used to store and access data that is kept over long periods of time.

Storage of data requires two components — the storage device and the storage media. First you need the storage device. The storage device writes the data onto the media and reads the data from the media. The second component is the storage media. This is the component that actually holds the data. Remember, the device reads and writes the data while the media holds the data.

There are two basic techniques for reading, writing, and storing data. One technique uses magnetic technology while the other uses optical technology. Each technique and the storage media that uses it will be covered. First we need to discuss the idea of data as it pertains to long term storage.

Data

Bits	Bytes or Characters	Fields	Records		Files
1	J	Jim Jones	Jim Jones		Student File
0	i	109 E. Main St.	.		
1	m	Dallas	.		
0 =	J =	Texas	= Mike Jones	= Instructor File =	Database
0	o	65771	.		
	n		.		
	e		Bill Miller		Class File
	s		.		
			.		

As discussed briefly in Lesson 3, data is stored in memory using magnetic digits called *bits*. The patterns of the bits are used to create numbers in a *binary* format. A certain number of bits, usually eight, make up a *byte* of data. Normally one character of data is stored in each byte. Storage media uses the same concept. When a character of data is stored on the storage media, it is stored in a byte that is composed of several bits.

When characters are combined to form a meaning, or describe part of an object, they are called *fields*. For example, characters are used to form your name but your name is part of what describes you. All the characters that make up your name are stored in a *field*. Fields are composed of characters that form a meaning. Other examples of fields would be your address, your age, your sex, or any other unit of data that you need to store about yourself.

If we take all the fields that describe you, we would have a *record*. A record contains all the stored information about a particular person, place, thing, or event. Records are composed of fields. If we wanted to store information about several people, each person would have his or her own record with each record having the same fields.

When we take all the records that contain the same kind of data and store them together, they are called a *file*. For example, we may have a file of all students in a school, a file of all items in an inventory, or a file of all houses in a city. Files are composed of records that contain like data. = files

All data that is stored together is referred to as a file. For example, if you created a term paper, the term paper would be stored in a file. It may not be apparent that the file consists of records, as described above, but technically it does. If it helps to understand the concept, think about each line in the term paper as being a record. When all lines are stored together, they are stored in a file.

The final step is to take different files that contain data that is related to each other in some way and combine them into a *database*. For example, in a school, you have teachers, students, and classes. Each of these three types of items would be stored in its own file. If we store all three files together, they would be considered a database.

BUILDING BLOCKS OF DATA

■ **Bit:** Single binary digit used to represent the presence or absence of a magnetized spot.

■ **Byte:** Series of bits, usually eight, used to store a single unit of data, usually one character.

■ **Field:** Series of bytes (characters) used to represent one characteristic of the stored data, like a person's name or address.

■ **Record:** Series of fields used to represent all data about a single person, place, thing, or event being stored. Each student would have his or her own record.

■ **File:** Group of records that contain like data about like objects. All student records would compose a file.

■ **Database:** Several files stored together that are related in some way.

These terms and concepts may appear to be simple, but they are extremely important when discussing data storage.

Magnetic Storage Devices and Media

One data storage technique uses magnetic technology. When using magnetic storage technology, the media is covered with a thin coating of material that can be magnetized. The material most commonly used is iron oxide. On these media, spots are magnetized in a precise pattern. The magnetized spots then become the bits in the binary numbers that represent the data. Normally, each pattern of magnetized spots, or byte of data, represents a character.

One of the major advantages of magnetic storage media is that the data can be erased. This allows the media to be erased and reused to store different data or to change existing data. Magnetic media and devices are also fairly inexpensive. This advantage, however, is also a disadvantage. Since the data can be erased, it can be accidentally destroyed. Magnetic storage media can also be damaged by the environment and other devices that have magnetic fields, like electric motors.

The devices that encode the data on magnetic media contain a *read/write head*. As implied by the name, a read/write head can both read the data from the media and write the data to the media. During the reading process, the heads detect the magnetized spots on the media and transfer their image into the computer's memory. During the writing process, the heads transfer an image of the data in primary memory and magnetize the bits on the media. The device and the media work together to store the data.

Magnetic Diskettes and Disk Drives

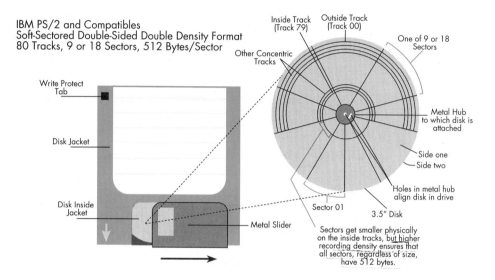

IBM PS/2 and Compatibles
Soft-Sectored Double-Sided Double Density Format
80 Tracks, 9 or 18 Sectors, 512 Bytes/Sector

Inside Track (Track 79)
Outside Track (Track 00)
Other Concentric Tracks
One of 9 or 18 Sectors
Write Protect Tab
Disk Jacket
Metal Hub to which disk is attached
Side one
Side two
Disk Inside Jacket
Holes in metal hub align disk in drive
Sector 01
3.5" Disk
Metal Slider
Sectors get smaller physically on the inside tracks, but higher recording density ensures that all sectors, regardless of size, have 512 bytes.

Magnetic disks are the most common storage media. These disks are made up of a base material that helps the disk maintain a rigid or semi-rigid surface. The surface of the disk is then coated with an iron oxide material.

2. The data is stored by magnetizing particles around concentric circles formed on the disks. These circles are called *tracks*. The function of the track is to store the data. In addition, the tracks are divided into pie-shaped sections called *sectors*. The function of the sector is to give points along the track that can be located by the device's read/write heads. Once a disk is set up to store data, it will have a limited number of tracks and each track will have a limited number of sectors.

6. When most disks are originally purchased, the tracks and sectors are not set up. This is because different computer systems and different *operating system software* requires a different number of tracks and sectors. Before a disk can store data it must be *formatted*. The process of *formatting* sets up the tracks and sectors on the disk. This formatting process is performed by the operating system software.

Data and Storage Devices

The devices that read and write data on the disks are referred to as _disk drives._ The disk drives work similarly to the way a stereo record or compact disk works on a modern stereo system. The read/write head is mounted on a movable arm. These heads float approximately 1/1000 of an inch above the disk. When data from a specific track is needed, as determined by the software, the disk begins to rotate and the arm moves the read/write head over the correct track. The read/write head waits for the correct sector to rotate beneath it. When the correct sector is found, the data is read and transferred into memory.

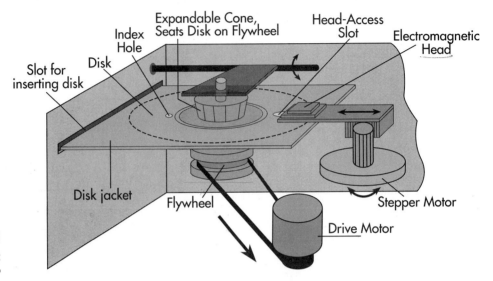

An internal floppy drive

Since the read/write heads can move directly to any track, the data on the diskette can be accessed randomly. When we say the data is accessed randomly, we mean that you do not need to process the data on the first track before you can process the data on the second or third track. The read/write heads can be moved directly to the track that contains the data. This ability makes the magnetic disk a _direct access device._ This direct access ability allows disk drives to store and locate data much faster than some other storage devices.

There are two categories of magnetic disk drives — diskette drives and hard disk drives. Diskette drives use removable diskettes as their storage media. Diskette drives accept one of two types of diskettes.

The first, and older type of drive uses a 5 1/4 inch _floppy disk_ as its storage media. This type of diskette is called a floppy disk because it is not rigid. It is flexible and will bend or _flop_. The disk itself is enclosed in a vinyl casing to protect the surface of the disk. The casing has a _hub_ or circular opening in the center. To get the disk to rotate so that it can be read, a spindle presses itself into the hub opening and begins to spin. This spins the diskette inside its vinyl case. There is also an opening in the vinyl case that gives the read/write heads access to the data on the disk.

On the right side of the diskette casing, there is a *write protect notch*. To protect the data stored on the disk from accidentally being erased or over-written, a small piece of tape can be placed over the notch. When the notch is taped, it is write protected. If the notch is not taped, the diskette can be written to or erased.

The second, and newer type of diskette is called a 3 1/2 inch diskette or *micro disk*. The disk itself is still a thin floppy disk, but it is enclosed in a hard, plastic casing. This hard casing provides more protection for the disk. Access to the disk is made through a sliding metal door on the top of the disk casing. When the diskette is inserted into the disk drive, a device pulls the door open. This gives the read/write heads access to the tracks on the disk.

4. The 3 1/2 inch micro disk has a *write protect switch* rather than a write protect notch like a 5 1/4 inch floppy disk. To protect the disk so that it cannot be erased, the switch is slid down so that you can see through the switch opening. If the switch is in the up position, so that the opening in the switch is covered, the disk can be erased and written to.

The exact amount of data that can be stored on a diskette depends on the number of sides used on the diskette, the format density, and the disk type. Most disk drives today can store data on both sides of the diskette. Diskettes that have been certified for use on both sides are labeled as DS (double sided). Some older diskettes may be labeled SS (single sided).

Disks can have different data densities. The data *density* of a diskette is determined by how close together the bits on the diskette can be stored. If the bits are closer together, more data can be stored on the diskette. The most common data densities for diskettes today are *double density* (DD) and *high density* (HD) High density diskettes store much more data than double density diskettes.

The 5 1/4 inch floppy disk can store 360,000 (360K) bytes of data when formatted for double density. If the diskette is formatted at high density, it can store 1.2 million (1.2MB) bytes of data. A 3 1/2 inch micro diskette can store 720,000 bytes of data when formatted at double density. If the 3 1/2 inch diskette is formatted for high density, it can store 1.44 million bytes (1.44 MB) of data.

5 1/4" FLOPPY DISKETTE

Double sided - Double density (DS-DD)	360,000 bytes of storage
Double sided - High density (DS-HD)	1,200,000 bytes of storage

ours →

3 1/2" MICRO DISKETTE

Double sided - Double density (DS-DD)	720,000 bytes of storage
Double sided - High density (DS-HD)	1,440,000 bytes of storage

The density of the diskette is determined by the capabilities of the disk drive and the formatting software.

High density disk drives can read and write double density diskettes, but double density disk drives cannot read and write high density diskettes.

Remember, the disk drive and the formatting software determine the disk's density, not the diskette itself. The technology of the disk drive determines the highest formatting the drive can process. High density disk drives can read and write diskettes formatted at double density, but double density disk drives cannot read and write diskettes formatted at high density diskettes. High density diskettes can be formatted for either double density or high density storage. Double density can normally only be formatted to store data at double density.

The 3 1/2 inch micro diskette will be the standard diskette for the microcomputer industry for several reasons. First, because of its harder casing and the protective door, this diskette is better protected. Second, it stores more data than the 5 1/4 inch diskette. Finally, it is smaller and easier to handle, transport, and store. A 3 1/2 inch diskette will easily fit into your pocket. Although the 3 1/2 inch diskette is expected to be the standard for some time to come, manufacturers are working on 2 1/2 inch and 1.8 inch diskettes that store twice as much data as the high density 3 1/2 inch diskette.

CONSUMER TIPS FOR CARE OF DISKETTES

- Don't touch the recording surfaces of the diskette.

- Keep diskettes away from electric motors and other devices that use magnetic fields.

- Do not bend, paper clip, or write directly on the diskette. Use a felt tip pen and light pressure when writing on the diskette's label.

- Keep away from direct sun light, excessive heat, and excessive cold.

- Store in protective envelopes or protective cases.

- Keep both the diskettes and the disk drives away from smoke and other pollutants.

- Label all diskettes with an indication of the data that is stored on them.

- Write protect diskettes that have information you don't want destroyed.

Hard or Fixed Disks

ours has 40 mega bytes

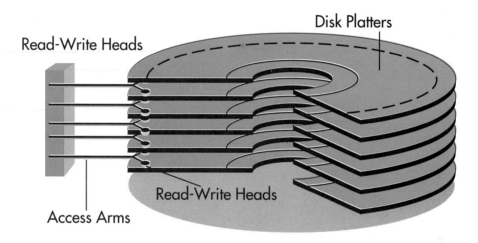

Read-Write Heads

Disk Platters

Read-Write Heads

A hard disk   Access Arms

One of the problems with diskettes is their storage capacity. 1.44 million bytes of data may seem to be a large amount of storage, but it isn't. Many software programs are larger than this, and it is not uncommon to have data files that require 10 or 20 million bytes of disk space. If a file were 10 million bytes long, you would need seven high density diskettes to store the file. Trying to determine which record was stored on which disk would be near impossible. Because of this storage problem, most microcomputers now have hard disks. Because the disks are not removable, like diskettes, *hard disks* are often called *fixed disks*.

Hard disks use the same basic technology as the diskette, i.e. formatting, tracks, sectors, etc., but they store much more data and retrieve the data much faster. Larger hard disks actually contain more than one recording platter. The more recording platters a drive has, the more data it can store.

With diskette drives, the disk only rotates when it is being read from or written to. On a hard disk the disk is always rotating. The read/write heads on a hard disk float approximately 1/1,000 of an inch above the disk surface. They never actually touch the surface of the disk. If they were to touch the surface of the disk, both the disk and the read/write heads could be damaged and become unusable. When this happens, it is commonly known as a *head crash*.

Hard disks have a very rigid recording platter. This rigid surface allows the data to be stored at a higher density. Storage capacities of hard disks range from 10 million bytes of storage up to three billion bytes (3 gigabytes). If an average hard disk drive had a capacity of 120 million bytes of storage, this would be equivalent to 167 double density or 84 high density 3 1/2 inch diskettes.

Because the hard disk is rigid and the read/write heads float above and below the disk platter, care must be taken when moving the disk drive. Bumps and jars to the disk drive may allow the read/write heads to bang into the disk which will cause dents and other types of damage. Before you move a computer having a hard disk you must *park* the read/write heads. Parking the heads makes them withdraw from the disk surfaces and locks them in place. Normally, parking the heads is performed by a software routine. Some of the newer hard disk drives have *auto park heads*. These drives automatically park the heads when the power is turned off.

Hard disks can either be internal drives, the most common, or they can be external. When the drive is internal, the only thing you will be able to see is the drive light. This light will come on when the drive is in use. If the drive is external, it will be enclosed in its own case and probably sit beside the main system cabinet.

Software storage requirements are growing as the software gets easier to use and performs more functions. To make the software easier to use, and to provide additional functions, more instructions are required in the program. As the size of the software grows and the amount of data being stored grows, the storage requirements will also grow. Not more than a few years ago, a 20 million byte hard disk was considered a large disk. Today, it is difficult to buy a 20 million byte hard disk. Eighty or 120 million byte hard disks are minimal in today's standards. These higher storage capacities are almost an absolute requirement for today's computer systems.

Magnetic Tape Media and Devices

Another common magnetic storage device is magnetic tape. On microcomputer systems, tape drives use either the standard cassette tape media or a mini cassette media. Larger mainframe and mini computer systems use both cassette and reel-to-reel tape drives.

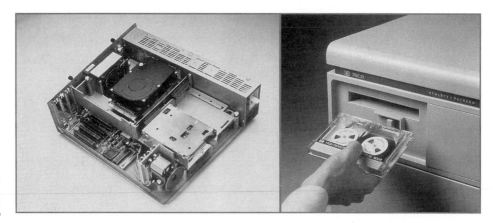

An internal and external tape drive

On magnetic tape data is stored as binary digits on *tracks,* but the tracks are horizontal and run the entire length of the tape, rather than being concentric circles like they are on disks. The data density of magnetic tape is determined by the closeness of the bits and the number of tracks on the tape.

The major advantage of magnetic tape systems is their high data density and their high storage capacity. Data densities on magnetic tape are measured in *bytes per inch* *(BPI).* Cassette tapes can store anywhere from several hundred million bytes up to one billion bytes (1 gigabyte) of data, depending upon the tape drive and the storage technique. Most tape drives will store data in a standard format or a *compressed format.* When data is stored in a compressed format, certain strings of characters are shortened or removed. For example, if you had 50 spaces at the end of a line, the compressed format would simply store the number 50 and the space character. This would result in only three bytes of storage used rather then 50 bytes. As a rule of thumb, compressed format requires one half the space of standard format.

The major disadvantage of magnetic tape is that it is a *sequential access device.* This means that access to the data on the tape must be performed in sequence, one record after another. Unlike disk drives, tape drives do not have the capability of moving the read/write heads directly to the data. This sequential access makes magnetic tape devices unacceptable for many common computer applications because access time to the data is too slow.

Because of its large storage capacity and slow data retrieval, magnetic tape is most commonly used as a backup media. When you *backup* data, you make a duplicate copy of the data. The reason you backup data is that you will have an extra copy in case the original copy is lost or damaged. Imagine that a 120 million byte hard disk was filled with important data. If, for some reason, the disk was damaged, you could lose access to all the data on the disk. You would need to use your backup to *restore* your data. If you tried to backup the 120 million byte hard disk on standard double density diskettes, it would take 167 diskettes and may take several hours. If you had a 250 million byte tape drive, you could backup the hard disk on a single cassette tape and still use only 1/2 of the tape's storage capacity. Using the tape drive to back up the data would probably only take 10 or 15 minutes.

Like hard disks, cassette tape drives may be internal or external. If they are internal, they normally take up an area where a diskette drive is used. With the large storage capacity of hard disks, it is becoming more common to have a tape back-up system on microcomputer systems.

Optical Storage Devices

The second technique used to store data uses an optical technology. When this technology is used, small indentations or *pits* are burned into the surface of a disk by a high power laser beam. Data is represented by the presence or the absence of the pit. The data is read by using a lower powered laser beam to reflect light from the pits. The absence or presence of the pit forms a *binary* image of the data.

This optical technology allows an enormous increase in the data density of the disk. Optical diskettes store between 550 and 1,000 million bytes of data. If a diskette using optical technology could store 550 million bytes of data, this would be equivalent to 764 3 1/2 inch double sided, double density, micro diskettes. Optical disks are also not affected by magnetic fields and other environmental contaminates like magnetic disks.

The primary disadvantage of optical technology, when compared to magnetic technology, is its data retrieval times. The time it takes to locate and retrieve a record on optical media is much longer than it is on magnetic media.

Like other storage devices, optical storage drives can be either internal or external.

CD-ROM

Could get external one - $300

A CD and CD-ROM drive

CD-ROM stands for *compact disk — read only memory*. This is the most common type of optical storage device. As the name implies, CD-ROM disks cannot be written to. They can only be read from. Storage capacities of CD-ROM disks range from 550 million bytes up to 1 billion bytes. Since the user cannot write to this diskette, one of its advantages is that the data cannot be accidentally erased.

The primary use of this type of media is for storing huge volumes of pre-recorded data. For example, you can buy a copy of an encyclopedia on CD-ROM. You get all the same data you would normally get in approximately 24 books, but it is on a single disk. Some other uses of CD-ROM are for legal references, medical references, and graphics libraries.

WORM

WORM stands for *write once — read many*. WORMs are a type of optical laser disk that can be written to by the user only once. Once data is recorded on a track, the track can only be read, never erased or changed.

This type of storage media is good in environments where large amounts of data must be recorded and kept forever, but the data will never change. For example, a city may want to keep records of land transfers. Using WORMs, all transfers would be kept and, over time, a history of the land ownership would be developed. A college or university may want to keep records of courses completed by students on WORMs. The college or university may be able to keep five or ten years of transcripts on a single WORM disk.

Erasable Optical Disk

An optical disk and disk drive

encyclopedias
profiles & records

In contrast to CD-ROMs and WORMs, erasable optical disks can be erased and rewritten to. These disks are relatively new, so they are not in wide use. These disks can be used as an alternative to large magnetic hard disks or as backup for large magnetic hard disks. An erasable optical disk can store from 280 million bytes up to several billion bytes of data.

Most experts expect optical storage will soon become the most efficient, inexpensive, and popular storage media. There are many optical drives on the market today, and some microcomputers already come with a CD-ROM disk drive as part of their standard equipment.

Using Storage Devices

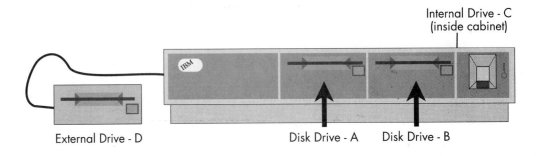

Internal Drive - C
(inside cabinet)

External Drive - D   Disk Drive - A   Disk Drive - B

Most microcomputers today have several storage devices. A typical microcomputer system will have either one or two diskette drives and one hard drive. Each of the drives will have a letter name that distinguishes the drive from the other drives attached to the machine. The drive letters are normally A, B, C, D, and so on depending on the number of drives you have.

In most cases, the two diskette drives are named the A and B drives. Also, in most cases, the hard disk drive is named the C drive. Even if you have only one diskette drive, the diskette drive will be named A drive and the hard disk drive will be named C drive. You would not have a B drive. You may also have a D drive that could be another hard disk or cassette drive. On some systems you may have only one physical hard disk drive; however, it may be set up as if it were two drives. In this case you would have both C and a D hard disk drive letters. This may sound a little confusing, but don't worry. Understanding the disk drive lettering system is easy once you have a little experience.

If you were to buy a computer today, it would probably be to your advantage to get one 5 1/4 inch diskette drive, one 3 1/2 inch disk drive, and a hard drive with at least 120 million bytes of storage. The reason for getting both sizes of diskette drives is because most older software comes on 5 1/4 inch floppy diskettes. Some newer software comes only on 3 1/2 inch micro diskettes. Having both drives will allow you to use software no matter what type of diskette it is on. You should also get high density disk drives. The price difference between high density and double density is insignificant. Remember, high density drives can process both high and double density diskettes.

Backup and Data Security

No discussion of data and storage devices would be complete without some mention of backup and data security. You must remember data is a valuable resource. It takes much time and expense to create the data. If the data is lost or damaged, it must be recreated. In some cases, it may not be possible to recreate the exact data. In the best case, it would be difficult.

Because data can be lost or destroyed, it is important to always make backup copies. As mentioned earlier in this lesson, a backup copy is simply a duplicate copy of the data. There is only one rule as to how often a backup copy should be made. To understand the rule, remember that if data is lost, it must be recreated. So, backup your data often enough so that the data that might be lost is only as much as you are willing to recreate. This should indicate that data should be backed up often.

Security of the diskettes is also important. Although you may have a backup copy, the diskette must be protected. Keep diskettes in a cool, dry area away from magnetic fields and environmental pollutants. Never keep your backup copies on the same disk or diskette as your original copy. This is a common careless error. If you were to lose the diskette or the diskette was to become unreadable, you would lose the original and the backup copy. Keep backup copies in a different physical location than the original. In some cases, a different room may be satisfactory. In other cases, a different building might be more appropriate. Remember, fires, floods, and other disasters do happen. If you keep your backup diskettes in the same box as the original copies, you are inviting disaster.

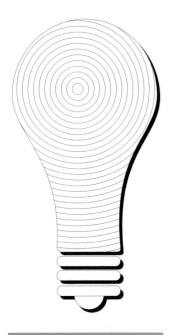

Summary

- The building blocks of data are bits, bytes, fields, records, files, and database.

- The two components to data storage are the storage media and the storage device. The device reads and writes the data while the media actually holds the data. The technology used by the media and the device may be magnetic or optical.

- Magnetic media includes floppy disks, micro disks, hard or fixed disks, and magnetic tape. The advantage of magnetic media is that it is erasable and can be reused. It is also fairly inexpensive. The disadvantage of magnetic media is that it can be damaged by magnetic fields and other environmental factors.

- Optical technology provides much higher data density than magnetic technology. In addition, it is not affected by magnetic fields and other environmental factors. It is relatively expensive when compared to magnetic storage.

- CD-ROM, WORM and erasable optical disks use optical technology.

- When multiple storage devices are on a single system, they are lettered. The letter names of the devices are A, B, C, D, etc., depending upon the number of devices. Diskette drives are usually lettered A and B. Hard drives and optical drives are usually lettered C and D drives.

- Data is an important resource. It must be backed up frequently. This backup should be on a different device and stored in a different location.

Review Questions

Answer the following questions to check your understanding of the lesson material.

1. List the six building blocks of data in order from smallest to largest.

2. Data is stored on a diskette on concentric circles called _____ that are divided into pie shaped areas called _____.

3. What capability of a disk drive allows the drive to directly access the data?

4. How do you write protect a 5 1/4 inch and a 3 1/2 diskette? What does write protecting do?

5. What determines the data density of a diskette?

6. What happens when a diskette is formatted?

7. List two advantages of a hard or fixed disk.

8. List one advantage and one disadvantage that magnetic tape has over a magnetic hard disk.

9. List two advantages that optical storage has over magnetic storage.

10. What advantage does WORM storage have over CD-ROM storage?

11. If you had two diskette drives and one hard drive on a microcomputer, what would the name of each drive be?

12. How often should you back up data?

6

Communicating With Other Computers

Learning Objectives

- Give an example of a digital system.

- Give an example of an analog system.

- Show how a modem is used and what its function is.

- Explain the difference between an internal and external modem.

- Describe how the speed of a modem is calculated.

- State some of the types of information available using commercial information services.

- Define uploading and downloading and give an example of each.

- Draw a diagram of several major types of LANs.

- State two advantages and disadvantages for each type of LAN.

- Compare the use of a LAN with the use of a modem.

Computers allow us to process all kinds of different information quickly and easily. However, often we need information that is not available on our own system. The information that we need is located on a different computer across the hall, or perhaps across the country. The ability to work with information from these other sites can dramatically expand our individual computing horizons.

The ability to link or *network* your personal computer can provide you with access to information services like Compuserve or Prodigy. Such services allow you to do everything from purchasing an airline ticket to looking up a topic in an encyclopedia. You could also monitor the stock market to track investments or have an electronic dialog with people around the world concerning the latest sports event.

You might find yourself connected to a network in your office where information is shared among all workers. You won't have to go to the file cabinet to find information for a customer since you can call up an electronic picture of the file from a CD-ROM optical disk on the network. If another office across the country needs the information, you can send it instantly at the touch of a button. Many workers will find that they will work at home and connect to the main office through a phone line.

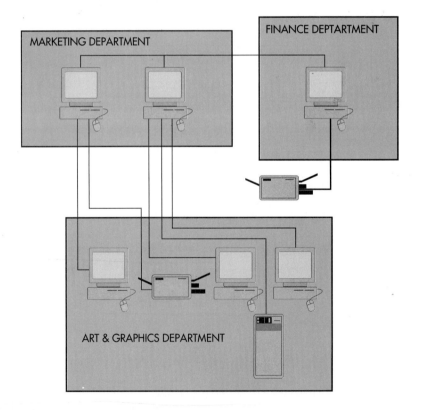

MARKETING DEPARTMENT

FINANCE DEPTARTMENT

ART & GRAPHICS DEPARTMENT

A typical
LAN configuration

Libraries connect to each other on a network so a user at one location can see holdings at all of the libraries. Many people can even "go to the library" from their homes though their computer. This will reduce the cost for the library and the user since all libraries won't have to carry all the material but rather can share material between other libraries on the network.

All of these activities are using data communications; that is, sending information from one computer to another. There are several ways that computers can be connected together. Often, computers are connected through regular telephone lines with a special device called a modem; this process is called telecommunications. Computers can also be connected in the same building or other small geographic areas using cables and are said to share a Local Area Network or LAN.

Telecommunications

Telecommunications allow two or more computers to be connected by regular telephone lines. This process works just like two people talking (or being connected) over the telephone lines for a voice conversation. The biggest difference between people using the phone (a *voice call*) and computers using the phone (a *data call*) is that the telephone network was designed to accommodate people talking, not computers. *talking*.

Using the Modem

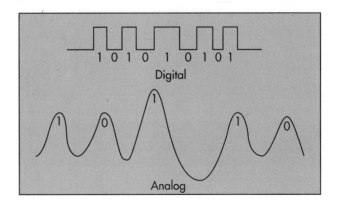

Digital versus analog

You should recall that computers operate on the binary principle where data is represented by a series of 1's and 0's. This is called (digital representation) since the only value a bit can have is a 0 or 1. People, however, talk using sounds or frequencies as their voices rise and fall. The sound waves vary continuously and are an (analog representation) of information.

This means that before the computer can communicate on the telephone lines, the computer's digital 1's and 0's have to be converted into analog sounds that the telephone system can understand. This conversion is done by a device called a MODEM which is short for MOdulate / DEModulate.

How the Modem Works

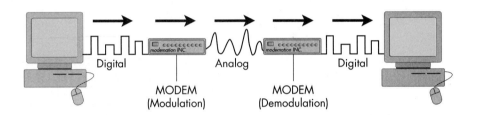

| Digital | MODEM (Modulation) | Analog | MODEM (Demodulation) | Digital |

Modems are serial devices since they must transmit or receive one bit at a time (see Lesson 3 for a review of serial devices). When transmitting data, the computer sends the modem one bit of data at a time. The modem takes this digital bit (1 or 0) and converts it into analog sound that the telephone system transmits. This process is called *modulation*. At the receiving computer, the modem receives the analog sound and demodulates it back into a digital bit (1 or 0).

Remember that modems convert the digital information from the computer into sound like our voices. The sound is then sent over the phone lines just like a normal voice conversation and converted back to digital information by the modem on the other end. This means that both the sending and the receiving computer must use modems when communicating over telephone lines. Finally, when the modem is in use, your telephone line will be busy, just as if you were making a voice call on the line. If you need to talk on the phone and connect to another computer through the modem at the same time, you will need an additional phone line.

Types of Modems

Modems are available in an external form that plugs into your computer's serial port or you can purchase a modem as an internal expansion card that plugs into

---

Learn PC Computer Literacy

an expansion slot in the system unit. The external modem has a series of indicator lights that make it somewhat easier to be sure you are connected. However, the internal modem is often less expensive. Both modems have a standard modular connection for a regular phone line. When purchasing either type of modem, be sure that it is Hayes compatible. This standard is the most widely accepted for personal computers and will ensure that you can easily connect to other systems.

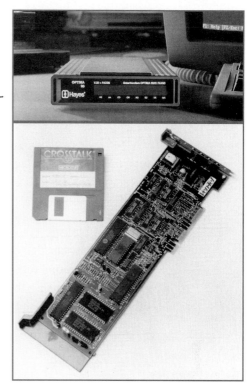

An external (top) and internal (bottom) modem

Modem Speeds

Modems come in different speeds with faster modems being able to send information over telephone lines at a faster rate. The speed of the modem is rated by the number of bits per second (bps) that it can send. Common modem speeds include 300, 1200, 2400, 4800, and 9600 bps capabilities. When you purchase a modem, it is best to get the fastest that you can afford since even fast modems operate much slower than the rest of the computer. Furthermore, faster modems can slow down to communicate with slower modems should the need arise. Probably the 2400 bps modem is the slowest that should be considered.

Uploading and Downloading Information

One of the exciting things you can do when you connect with a modem to another computer or information service is to send or receive information over the telephone lines. When you get some information from the computer you are connected to, it is called downloading. If you send information up to the other computer, it is referred to as uploading.

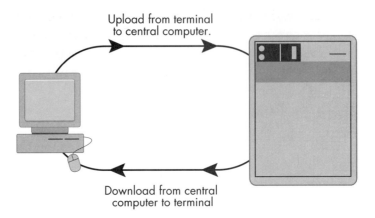

Upload from terminal
to central computer.

Download from central
computer to terminal

All kinds of information is available on electronic bulletin boards and information services including entire programs for games, word processing, and much more. What's more, most of these are available free of charge. The best way to gain experience using this powerful tool is to find a local bulletin board or to subscribe to one of the national computer information services such as *Compuserve*, *Genie*, or *Prodigy*.

Network Concepts

The use of a modem allows you to connect to other computers over phone lines, but even with a fast modem, the speed at which information is sent is slow. To allow computers to share large amounts of information and programs, much higher speeds are required and provided by a local area network or LAN.

Local Area Networks

Local area networks are installed in some specific geographic area like a building or a campus giving rise to the name "local." Instead of using telephone lines and modems to connect computers, special cables are installed which serve to connect the various computers. These cables allow information to be transmitted in a digital format directly between computers so modems are not required. By not having to convert the information from digital to analog with a modem, much higher speeds are possible; in fact, many LANs operate at 4 or even 10 million bits per second. This is certainly much faster than the 9600 bps speed of even a fast modem.

Each computer that is attached to the network must be equipped with a special network expansion card that is placed inside the computer system unit. Special network software is also installed in the computer; this allows the computer user to connect to the network easily. In fact, many network users find that the network is *transparent* to them which means that they can get needed information from the network without ever worrying about special network commands.

LAN File Servers

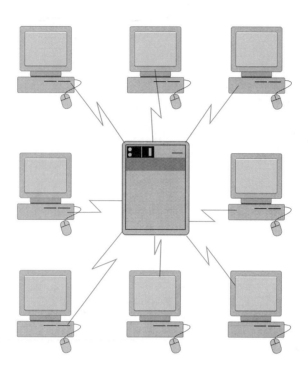

A star network configuration

The main benefit from the use of a network is the ability to share information and programs with other users. To make information sharing easy, most LANs use a large personal computer called a *file server* as a central holding area where programs and information are kept. Other connected computers, called *nodes*, can access programs and information on the file server whenever it is needed. The file server appears to the individual nodes as a separate hard disk that is accessible from their computer.

When the file server is accessed by all users, it is easy to share expensive resources like laser printers or special programs since many users can use them effectively. By keeping one copy of information in the file server rather than many different copies stored in separate computers, the information will be more up-to-date and accurate. This is because the same information is used by everyone on the LAN. It is also easier to back up data and information on the file server since it is in one place, rather than spread across many machines. To prevent problems, LAN software can control who can access information and what changes can be made to it.

When LANs were first available, it was difficult to find software that would make full use of the network capabilities. This problem has vanished as software developers have created special LAN features that make using the LAN easy. These special LAN versions of word processors, spreadsheets, and other programs, allow multiple users to use one software package at the same time. Many software firms offer site licenses which allows all computer users in the organization to use the software package for one discounted price. These special software arrangements help to control problems of software piracy, and backup; they also ensure that the latest version of the program is in use across the organization.

LAN Configurations

Local area networks can be arranged in many different ways, but the most common are the bus, star, and ring configurations. These configurations refer to the way the overall network would look if you could stand over it and look down at the entire LAN.

The Bus LAN

The bus LAN is designed with a single, common wire or *bus* that connects all the devices on the network. The bus network is easy to install and add stations to later on. It also offers powerful performance and is widely accepted by users. The file server can be located in any position on the bus and provides considerable flexibility in the LAN design. The biggest potential problem with bus systems is that when many users (several hundred) are connected to the LAN, the speed at which the LAN operates will decline.

The Star Network

The star LAN configuration differs from the bus in that there is a central location housing the file server, and other users radiate out from it. This LAN is more difficult to install than the bus but is very easy to maintain since each PC or node is connected to the server with its own cable. If one cable breaks, it does not affect any of the other computers on the LAN.

The Ring LAN

The last type of LAN is designed in a continuous ring format. This allows the LAN to perform very well under conditions of heavy use or when many users are connected to it. Under heavy-use conditions, it is preferred to the bus or star LAN design. However, the ring design is typically the most costly LAN because of the more expensive expansion cards that are needed. In the ring design, the file server can be located in any position.

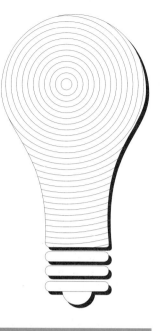

Summary

Modem Requirements

- Data that is represented in both digital form (using 1's and 0's) for use by computers and analog form where frequencies are used for normal voice communications.

- Modems can be purchased as either internal expansion card models or external models that plug into the computer's serial port.

- Modems must be used to convert the computer's digital signals into the analog signal used by the phone for communications. Modems come in a variety of speeds which are measured in the number of bits per second that can be transmitted over the phone lines.

- Even the fastest modem operates much slower than any other part of the computer.

Local Area Networks

- Local area networks (LANS) can connect nearby computers at high rates of speed over private cables.

- The information is transmitted in a digital format and operates many times faster than modem communications.

- LANs are easy to use and are available in several configurations with the bus, ring, and star being the most popular.

Information Services

- Through computer communications, you can connect to many different information services and sources.

- Services including *Prodigy*, *Compuserve*, *Genie*, and others allow you to access huge volumes of information at a low monthly cost. This ability can dramatically increase the power of your computer and makes using your computer more fun.

Review Questions

Answer the following questions to check your understanding of the lesson material.

1. What kind of signal does the computer understand?

2. What type of transmission was the telephone system designed to use?

3. What does the word MODEM stand for?

4. What is the purpose of having a modem?

5. Where does an external modem connect to the computer?

6. How are modem speeds determined?

7. If you wanted to receive an information file from a host computer, you would _____ it.

8. What are two major advantages a LAN has when compared with modem use?

9. Name the three most common LAN designs:

   _____   _____   _____

10. Name two commercial information services.

System Software

Learning Objectives

- Distinguish between system software and application software.

- Understand what an operating system does.

- List several functions of an operating system.

- List several characteristics of different PC and PC-compatible operating systems.

- To understand the reason for software versions and the version numbering system.

- Define the terms compiler, interpreter, operating system, multitasking, virtual memory, DOS, OS/2, UNIX, System 7, Windows, and software version.

n this lesson you will learn about computer software. Without computer software the computer hardware would be useless. Computer software allows your computer system to operate and control its hardware as well as allowing you to create letters and reports, plan your financial affairs and evaluate different alternatives, produce graphs and drawings, play games, learn new skills, and accomplish an endless variety of tasks with your computer.

What Is Software?

Computer software is a program, or set of programs, that tell the computer hardware (input, processor, output, and storage devices) how to perform certain tasks. A computer program is a detailed set of instructions that tell the computer the precise sequence of steps that must be taken to perform a task. The term software comes from the fact that you cannot touch the instructions. The instructions are stored as codes on a disk or in memory. This is in contrast to hardware which is the equipment that you can touch.

This definition of computer software is very narrow. A much broader definition of software would include the programs, manuals, warranty, upgrade policy, training, and user support provided by the manufacturer of the software. In this lesson we will stay with the traditional, more narrow, definition of software but you need to remember that the other components are necessary to make effective use of the software.

System Software

There are two general categories or classes of computer software — system software and application software. System software consists of the operating systems that control the hardware of the computer system, language translators, and other utility programs that help the computer perform its basic tasks. The system software coordinates the operations of all the hardware components.

Application software are programs that are designed to solve specific business, personal, or professional tasks. For example, word processing software allows the user to create reports, and documents. Graphics software allows the user to create charts, drawings, and artwork.

Remember, the systems software allows the computer to perform its basic tasks and control its hardware. The application software allows the user to perform job-related tasks.   #2

Programming and Programming Languages

As mentioned earlier, programs are a sequence of instructions that tell the computer what to do. These programs are written by people called programmers. Programmers define the logic needed to accomplish a task and then write the instructions in a specific programming language.

There are hundreds of programming languages. You have probably heard of some of the languages like BASIC, COBOL, FORTRAN, PASCAL, C, and others. All languages are capable of performing the same general types of operations, but each language has been designed to make certain types of applications easier to write. The languages use different words and terms, but they are all written in some form of English. Since the computer cannot interpret the English language directly, these English-like statements must be translated into computer or machine language. This translation process is performed by other system software called *compilers* or *interpreters*. The function of both compilers and interpreters is to translate a program written in an English-like programming language into machine language.

As you learn more about computers you may want to learn more about programming, but you do not need to understand programming to use software. Most software is written to be used by novice users.

Operating Systems

Operating systems are system software. The function of the operating system is to coordinate and manage all the different operations that occur in the computer system. These operations include coordinating processing tasks, managing memory, managing use of the disk and disk drive, managing the flow of information to and from the input and output devices, and checking for and displaying errors.

System Software   113

4

SOME FUNCTIONS OF THE OPERATING SYSTEM

- Coordinating processing

- Managing memory

- Coordinating disk operations

- Managing use of the disk and disk drive

- Coordinating the flow of information to and from the input and output devices

- Checking for and displaying errors

The operating system is actually a set of programs. One of the programs in the operating system, called the *supervisor,* is immediately loaded into memory when the computer is started. This program allows you to use the computer and access the other utility programs that are part of the operating system. These utility programs perform many of the more specific tasks necessary for you to use your disks and disk drives. For example they may allow you to format a diskette, check a disk for errors, and copy or delete files.

There are several operating systems available for different types of computer systems. The most common operating systems for IBM-PC and PC compatible systems are PC-DOS, MS-DOS, OS/2, and UNIX.

SOME FUNCTIONS OF THE OPERATING SYSTEM UTILITY PROGRAMS

- Format a diskette

- Check a diskette for bad tracks

- List the files on a disk

- Copy files from one disk to another

- Delete files from a disk

- Create directories and subdirectories

- Set the current date and time

- Sort data

- Recover lost data

- Customize the way your computer operates

- Compare files and diskettes
- Search for a file
- Show the operating system version
- Print a file
- Rename a file

PC-DOS and MS-DOS

DOS stands for *disk operating system*. PC-DOS was developed by IBM and is used on IBM brand microcomputers. MS-DOS is owned by the Microsoft Corporation and is used on IBM compatible computers. There is actually little difference between the two operating systems, so if you know how to use one, then you generally know how to use the other.

These two operating systems are *command driven* operating systems. This means that you type a command to the operating system to get it to accomplish a certain task. For example, if you wanted to copy a file named **EXERCISE.TXT** from the A drive to the C drive, you would type:

```
COPY A:EXERCISE.TEXT C:EXERCISE.TXT
```

To use one of the disk operating systems, you must learn a large number of commands and learn the *syntax* of each command. The term *syntax* stands for sentence structure and means that each command must be written in a precise format or order. Most users only need to learn a few commands available in DOS in order to use the computer system.

The newer versions of DOS, DOS 5.0 and above, includes a program called the *DOS SHELL* that allows you to use most of the DOS commands through a menu system. This shell program allows you to use a mouse. The DOS SHELL makes DOS easier to use. DOS 5.0 also provides a capability known as *task swapping*. Task swapping allows more than one program to run at the same time.

OS/2

Since you needed to learn a large number of commands and the syntax of each command when you used DOS, many people thought DOS was too cumbersome for the average microcomputer user. DOS also had a number of limitations that sophisticated users needed to overcome. Because of the complexity and limitations of DOS, IBM and Microsoft Corporation developed *OS/2* or Operating

System 2 to replace PC and MS-DOS. OS/2 and its accompanying *Presentation Manager* software allows the user to communicate with the operating system through a *graphical interface*. This graphical interface allows you to choose options from menus and icons rather than typing commands. This makes the system much quicker and easier to learn for the normal user.

OS/2 supports multitasking. Multitasking allows you to run more than one program at the same time, a limitation imposed by earlier DOS and known as *task swapping* in the later DOS versions. OS/2 also supports the concept of *virtual memory*. This means that the operating system can use part of a hard disk as if it were internal memory, effectively increasing the amount of RAM available to the system. OS/2 uses a *clipboard* technique that allows you to copy data easily from one application program to another. OS/2 can access more internal memory than DOS, thus making it easier to run large programs.

The disadvantage of OS/2 is that the operating system itself requires much more memory to be stored. It requires at least 4 million bytes of memory to run and requires at least a 386 processor to run effectively. Another disadvantage of OS/2 is that there are relatively few application programs that will run under the operating system, when compared to the application programs available for DOS.

UNIX

UNIX is another common operating system. It was developed by Kenneth Thompson at Bell Laboratories (AT&T). UNIX has two major advantages over both DOS and OS/2. First, UNIX supports a multi-user environment. This means that you can connect several monitors and keyboards to a single microcomputer processor. Each monitor and keyboard is considered a *terminal*. This allows several users to use the same CPU at one time. These users can share the same applications software, data files, disk drives, and other hardware.

The second major advantage of UNIX is that it is available for microcomputers and larger mini and mainframe computers. This allows a company with several different size computers to use the same operating system on all of its computers. If the users know UNIX on the microcomputer, they also know how to use the mainframe's operating system. Disadvantages of UNIX include its high cost and the lack of business application programs that will run properly with the operating system.

OPERATING SYSTEM	ADVANTAGE	DISADVANTAGE
PC and MS-DOS	Requires small amount of memory	Command driven except in version 5.0 using the DOS SHELL
	Works on 8088, 8086 80286, 80386, and 80486 processors	Allows only one user per computer
	Most common	Allows only one program at a time except in version 5.0
OS/2	Menu and icon driven	Requires a large amount of RAM (at least 4MB) and a hard disk
	Allows multitasking	Requires minimum 386 processor running at 20MHz to run effectively
	Supports larger memory capacities	Few application programs available
	Supports virtual memory	
	Easy to copy data between applications programs	
UNIX	Allows multitasking	Command driven
	Supports larger memory capacities	Requires a large amount of RAM (4MB) and a hard disk
	Supports multiple users	Expensive
	Supports multitasking	Lack of business application programs
	Available on micro-computer, minis, and mainframes	

Handwritten annotations:

Developed by :

IBM → *PC and MS-DOS*, *Microsoft* →

IBM and Microsoft (OS/2)

AT&T (UNIX)

Microsoft Windows is not an operating system. It is a software environment, developed by Microsoft Corporation, that can be used with DOS. Windows provides the user with a graphical user interface (much like OS/2). Windows also allows you to organize your computer screen into an electronic desktop, placing different applications in different areas of the screen.

To use Windows, you select icons or small pictures that represent the program or task you want to perform. For example, to run a program, you click your mouse on the program's icon rather than typing a RUN command like you would do in the older versions of DOS. All of the normal DOS commands are available to you when using Windows, but you choose the commands from menus rather than typing them.

Windows comes with many accessories, such as a calculator, clock, calendar, note pad, and drawing tools. These are electronic tools that you use on your screen rather than being separate hardware devices. Other features that are available in Windows are the File Manager, that allows you to locate and arrange files on your hard disk or diskettes; Program Manager, that organizes and allows you to run programs; Accessories, that provide access to the calculator and other extra windows tools; Control Panel, that allows you to set different features of Windows; and a Print Manager, that controls printing.

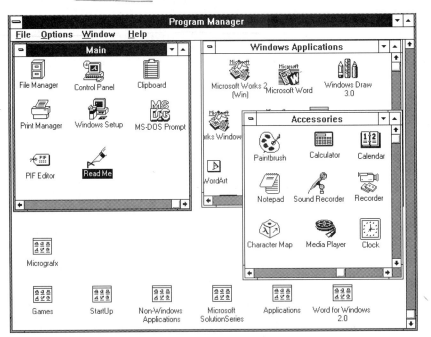

A Windows screen

Along with the advantage of the graphical interface, Windows allows you to run many programs at the same time and easily switch between programs. Using Windows, you can be working in a word processing program, switch to a graphic program to draw a picture, then copy the picture back to the word processing program.

System 7

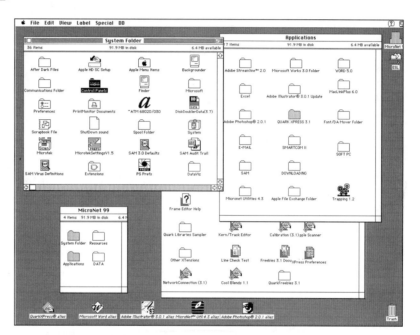

A Macintosh
System 7 screen

System 7 is an operating system for Apple Corporation's Macintosh line of micro-computers. Like OS/2 and Microsoft Windows, System 7 uses a graphical inter-face and a mouse to perform most of its operations. On a Macintosh using System 7, files are stored in areas called *folders*. To see what files are in a folder you simply use your mouse to point to the folder and click the mouse button. This opens the folder and makes all the files in it available to you. To run a pro-gram, you simply point to the program's icon and double click the mouse button.

System 7 will allow you to *link* data from one program to data in another pro-gram. When the original data is changed, the data in the programs that use the linked files are changed as well. System 7 also supports *virtual memory,* thus effec-tively increasing the amount of RAM available to the programs. System 7 and Microsoft Windows are similar in the way they work. The primary difference between the two is that System 7 is for Apple Macintosh computers and Windows is for IBM and IBM-compatible computers.

Operating System Versions and Compatibility

Remember that operating systems are programs written by human programmers. Programmers occasionally make mistakes that are translated to errors in the program or operating system. Also, remember that the operating system controls the computer hardware. Hardware is constantly being improved and new hardware is constantly being developed. For these reasons, operating systems are constantly being upgraded or improved to correct errors, improve performance, and support new hardware.

Operating systems and software manufacturers have adopted a numbering system to indicate these versions, or revisions, of the software. The numbering system consists of a decimal number with the first part indicating a major revision and the second part indicating a minor correction to the version. For example, version 1.0 will be the first version of an application program or operating system. When minor improvements and corrections are made, the version number will move up to version 1.1, 1.2, 1.3, etc. When major changes are made, the version number will change to 2.0, then to 2.1, 2.2, etc., until another major revision, 3.0, occurs. In general, the higher the number, the newer and more advanced the version of the software will be.

Application software is very dependent upon the operating system software. When a version of an application program is written, it is normally written for the most current version of the operating system. The newer application program may be using instructions that older versions of the operating system do not have. This means that newer versions of application software may not run correctly with older versions of the operating system. In general, application software can be moved forward to newer versions of an operating system, but they cannot be moved backwards. For example, if a program is written for version 3.0 of MS-DOS, it will probably run correctly under version 4.0 or 5.0, but it may not run correctly under version 2.0 or 1.0. Most application software will indicate the minimum version of the operating system required.

There are some exceptions to the upward mobility rule. For example, some Macintosh application software that worked correctly under System 6.0 will not work correctly under system 7.0; however, most of the software will move up.

SIDE NOTE: *Since software often contains errors that are corrected in later versions, many experienced users will tell you to never use version .0 of any software. Example: Don't buy 3.0 of any software since it will more than likely have bugs. Wait for version 3.1 or 3.2.*

Learn PC Computer Literacy

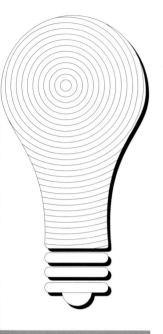

Summary

- Software consists of computer programs. A computer program is a detailed set of instructions that tell the computer the precise sequence of steps that must be taken to perform a task.

- System software controls the internal operation of the computer system and its hardware. System software consists of the operating system, compilers and interpreters, and system utilities.

- Interpreters and compilers translate high level English language into machine language.

- The operating systems coordinate processing, manage internal memory, control disk activity, control the flow of information to and from the input and output devices, and control error messages. There are four major operating systems for the IBM-PC and PC compatibles — PC-DOS and MS-DOS, OS/2, and UNIX.

- Microsoft Windows is an operating environment rather than an operating system. Windows uses icons and menus rather than commands to communicate with the operating system.

- System 7 is the predominate operating system for the Apple Macintosh line of computer systems.

- System software, like application software, is occasionally revised. Each revision has its own version number. The higher the software version number, the more recent the software. Normally you can change to a newer version of the software but you cannot change to an older version.

Review Questions

Answer the following questions to check your understanding of the lesson material.

1. Define the term software.

2. Distinguish between system software and application software.

3. Programmers write instructions in an English-like language that is converted to a machine language by a _____ or an _____.

4. List six functions of an operating system.

5. How do PC and MS-DOS differ from OS/2?

6. List two major advantages of UNIX over PC and MS-DOS.

7. Microsoft Windows is not an operating system. What is it?

8. What type of computer system uses the System 7 operating system?

9. Why are there different versions of operating systems and application software?

10. Explain how the version numbering system works for software.

Application Software

Learning Objectives

- Describe some of the common characteristics of word processing software.

- Describe some of the common characteristics of electronic spreadsheet software.

- Describe some of the common characteristics of database software.

- Describe three different types of graphics software.

- Describe the function of telecommunications software.

- List several different kinds of software utility programs.

- List three different ways to obtain software.

- List things you should consider when purchasing software.

- Explain what a computer virus is and how it is spread.

- List several signs of a computer virus.

#2

System software controls the hardware devices and internal operation of the machine. Application software allows you to perform certain types of jobs. For example, if you wanted to create a report, you would need some word processing applications software. If you wanted to graph sales data, you would need some graphing application software. There are hundreds of application software areas with many different software packages in each area. If there is a job that needs to be done, there is an application program that will help you do it.

The most commonly used application programs on a microcomputer are word processing, electronic spreadsheets, graphics, and database management programs.

APPLICATION SOFTWARE AREAS

Word Processing	Electronic Spreadsheets	Graphics
Desktop Publishing	Art and Drawing	Telecommunications
Computer Assisted Design (CAD)	Computer Assisted Manufacturing (CAM)	Education
Database	Presentation	Engineering
Utilities	Training	Mapping

Word Processing Programs

Word processing programs turn your computer into a sophisticated electronic typewriter. With word processing software you can create reports, memos, term papers, business and personal letters, posters, announcements, brochures, and almost any type of printed document. We will briefly discuss some of the capabilities of a word processing program but will not come close to covering all of its capabilities.

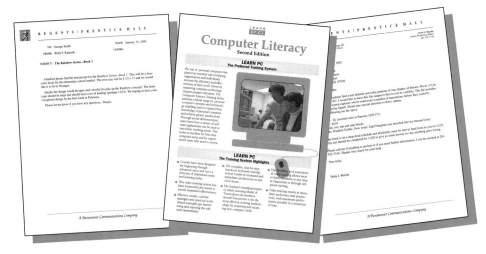

Several word processing documents

A word processing program presents you with a blank screen that is like a piece of blank paper. You then type on the keyboard just as if you were typing on a typewriter. If you make a mistake, you can use your backspace key or delete key to correct the mistake. Since the document is in RAM, and not printed as you type, there is no longer a need to use erasers or white-out to correct errors.

Once a document is typed, you can delete, move, or copy large segments of text. To delete a segment of text, you use a mouse or a series of special keystrokes to highlight the text; then press the delete key. When the text is deleted, the remaining text is moved to fill in the area where the deleted text was.

Deleting a paragraph in Microsoft Word

If you want to move text from one location to another, you select the text, choose a move operation from a menu, or use a function key. Next tell the program where you want the text moved. The text is deleted from its original location and inserted in its new location. This is sometimes referred to as a cut and paste operation.

You can also copy text from one location to another. This type of operation normally works like a move operation but the text is not deleted from its original location. This avoids typing the same text more than once.

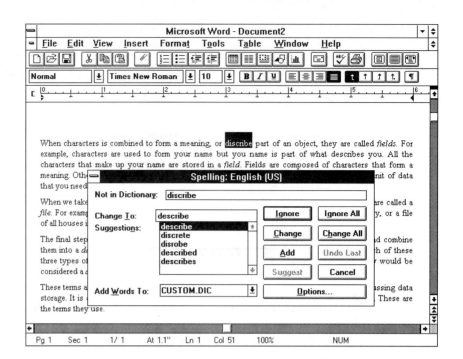

Spell check dialog box

Most word processing programs provide a spell checking feature and a thesaurus. The spell checking feature will check the spelling of each word in the document. When a spelling error is found, the word is presented along with several possible, correct spellings. You can select the correctly spelled word from the list of suggested spellings, and the word is automatically corrected.

The thesaurus will allow you to select alternative words (synonyms) for a particular word. You can use the thesaurus to find a word that more precisely represents the idea you are trying to convey. Using a thesaurus will also help you develop your own vocabulary.

Another feature of most newer word processing programs is a grammar checker. A grammar checker can evaluate your writing, checking for correct punctuation, sentence structure, and word usage. Grammar checkers will locate your possible errors, suggest what is wrong with the grammar, and suggest corrections.

Once you have the document entered and checked for spelling and grammar, you can change the look of the entire document or certain areas of the document. You can change the margins, indent certain areas, highlight text by making it bold, underlined or italicized, or change the font used for the text.

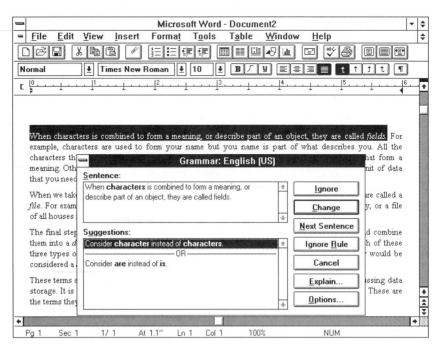

Grammar check
dialog box

Some word processing programs will allow you to place lines or *rules* between text to separate it or allow *borders* or boxes around the text. Most word processing programs will also allow you to create multiple columns and tables in a document much like newspapers and magazines.

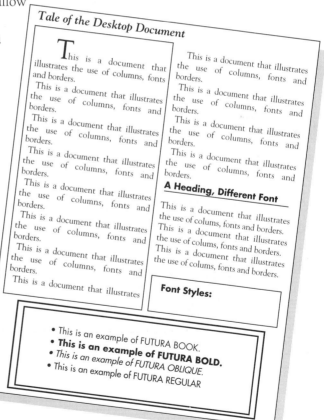

Two-column
document with
borders and
different fonts

Modern word processing programs provide a WYSIWYG (**W**hat **Y**ou **S**ee **I**s **W**hat **Y**ou **G**et) display of the document. This means that the screen displays the document exactly the way it will print. Some word processing programs will also allow you to insert graphics and artwork into the document. This feature can allow you to create advertisements and brochures. Another feature that is important in word processing programs is the ability to import documents that have been created by other programs. You may need this capability if you change from one word processing program to another.

There are many other features too numerous to mention. Suffice to say that a word processing program is an absolute necessity if you intend to create letters and documents with your computer. A word processing program is probably the first program you would want to get when you buy your own computer system. They can save endless hours of work. **Microsoft® Word**, **WordPerfect®**, **Wordstar** and **Mac Write** are popular word processing programs.

COMMON WORD PROCESSING FEATURES

Cut and Paste Operations	Spell Checking
Text Highlighting (bold, italics, and underline)	Thesaurus
Changeable Margins	Grammar Checking
Multiple Columns	Headers and Footers
Automatic Page Numbering	Footnotes
Page Preview	WYSIWYG
Changeable Print Fonts	Table of Contents
Indexing	Search and Replace text
Automatic Hyphenation	Borders and Rules
Print Merge with Databases	Style Sheets
Graphics	Import and Export to other programs

A type of applications software that is related to a word processing program is *desktop publishing* software. Desktop publishing software, often called page layout software, is similar to word processing software. They both manage text well. The advantage of desktop publishing software is its ability to handle graphic images and the arrangement of text on a page.

With desktop publishing software, you can insert almost any type of graphic image, scanned or drawn with graphics software, anywhere in a document. You can move the graphic image anywhere on a page. Most desktop publishing software also provides more ways to highlight and shape text. For example, you may be able to slant text to get certain effects or force shadows to occur on the text.

Using desktop publishing software, you can create your own catalogs and sales brochures, books and manuals, newsletters, and almost any other type of document that you used to produce by physically cutting and pasting pictures onto pages. In fact, this text and most other books you see today have been totally created using desktop publishing software on a microcomputer. Aldus Page Maker®, Ventura Publisher®, and Quark Xpress® are popular desktop publishing programs.

**Sales brochure
with graphics**

Electronic Spreadsheets

What word processing programs do for words, electronic spreadsheets do for numbers. Electronic spreadsheets allow you to enter your data and use formulas to calculate new data based upon the data you have entered. When you change a number in the spreadsheet, any other number that is based upon the one changed will be recalculated. One single change may force hundreds of recalculations and these recalculations could take place in seconds.

#5

A spreadsheet consists of a series of rows and columns. Rows are labeled with a number and columns are labeled with either one or two letters. Each point where a row and a column meet is called a cell. Data is entered in the cells of the spreadsheet. Each cell is identified by the column letter and the row number of the cell. For example, the first cell in a spreadsheet is in column A and row one, so it is referred to by the cell name A1. The next cell to the right would be cell B1, and the cell directly below this cell would be cell B2.

	A	B	C	D	E
					Sheet1
1					
2					
3					
4					
5					
6			Cell C6		
7					
8					
9					
10					

Empty spreadsheet pointing out cell coordinates

Spreadsheet cells can store three types of data — numbers, text, and formulas. Numbers or values are your raw data, the data that you know and enter directly. Text or labels help explain what the numbers represent. Formulas are used to calculate results based on your numbers. For example, if you had a price per item in cell A2 and the quantity you purchased in cell B2, you could compute the total cost by entering the formula =A2*B2.

This example is simple, but suppose you had a large list of the prices and quantities on which you needed to compute taxes. You could place all of these in a spreadsheet and have all the taxes computed. If the tax rate changed, one change to the spreadsheet could have all the taxes re-computed.

Spreadsheets have a large number of special formulas called *functions*. These functions allow you to compute financial data like payments on a loan, the future value of an investment, or depreciation of a business asset. There are also many math and scientific functions that will compute things like the tangent of two angles, the cosine of a number, or the logarithm of a number. These functions make it easier to perform more complex calculations.

Once a spreadsheet is set up and the data is stored in the spreadsheet, you can still insert new rows and columns into it. When the new rows and columns are inserted, all formulas and coordinates in the formulas are recalculated to reflect the location of the new rows and columns. Rows and columns can also be copied or moved much the same way data is moved in a word processing program.

	A	B	C	D	E
1	Tax Rate	4%			
2	Item	Price	Qty	Tax	Total
3	Diskettes	12.95	25	12.95	$336.70
4	Pencils	0.50	100	2.00	$52.00
5	Paper	10.95	10	4.38	$113.88
6	Note Books	5.00	15	3.00	$78.00
7	Paper Clips	1.95	5	0.39	$10.14
8	Pens	2.69	77	8.29	$215.42

Before Change of Tax Rate

	A	B	C	D	E
1	Tax Rate	5%			
2	Item	Price	Qty	Tax	Total
3	Diskettes	12.95	25	16.19	$339.94
4	Pencils	0.50	100	2.50	$52.50
5	Paper	10.95	10	5.48	$114.98
6	Note Books	5.00	15	3.75	$78.75
7	Paper Clips	1.95	5	0.49	$10.24
8	Pens	2.69	77	10.36	$217.49

After Change of Tax Rate

Spreadsheet showing instant change of data

Another feature of a spreadsheet is the *macro*. A macro allows you to enter a series of commands in the spreadsheet and store them as a single keystroke. Once the macro is created, it can reproduce all the commands with the single keystroke. This can dramatically reduce the time it takes to set up a spreadsheet or execute a frequently used series of keystrokes. Macros are also available in most word processing and database programs.

Most electronic spreadsheets also allow you to create *templates*. A template is a spreadsheet where all the formulas have been stored, but the raw data is not stored. To create a new spreadsheet, you can use the template. All you would need to enter is the raw data, not the formulas. Once you enter your data, all the formulas will calculate data for additional cells. Using templates, you can create within minutes a spreadsheet that contains hundreds of entries. Like macros, templates can also be created in word processing and database programs.

Once you have the data in the spreadsheet, you can style the data in the spreadsheet with different formats. For example, you could have the numbers printed with commas and dollar signs, or you could have the data rounded to the nearest penny. In many spreadsheet programs you can change the size and font used for the data. Once the spreadsheet is completed and formatted the way you want it, you can print the entire spreadsheet or only part of it. Most spreadsheet software will also create simple presentation graphics from the data.

Spreadsheet software is used by business people to help with financial planning, accounting and bookkeeping people to help keep records, scientists to help analyze research data, teachers to help keep track of grades, and almost anyone who needs to deal with large volumes of numbers. An electronic spreadsheet is probably the second most commonly used software program on a microcomputer system. Popular spreadsheet programs include **Lotus® 1-2-3**, **Quattro Pro**, and **Microsoft® Excel**.

COMMON FEATURES OF AN ELECTRONIC SPREADSHEET

Automatic and Manual Recalculation	Table Look Up Procedures
Copy and Move Rows and Columns	Insertion and Deletion of Rows and Columns
Formulas and Functions	Cell Protection
Print all or part of the Spreadsheet	Macros
Cell Formatting	Templated
Search and Replace	Presentation Graphics
Automatic Filling of Cells	And many more

Database Software

Our society has developed an insatiable appetite for information. We just cannot get enough of it. We have collected and stored so much information that it can no longer be managed manually. Database software helps store, retrieve, update, and report data that has been stored electronically on a database.

You are probably familiar with the most common database, a telephone book. The only difference between a telephone book and a computer database is that the computer database is stored electronically rather than in printed form. This electronic storage of the data allows you to use the power and speed of the computer to process the data. In fact, when you call an operator requesting a phone number, the operator uses an electronic phone book to find it.

A database is composed of files or in some cases a single file. If we use the example of a telephone book, the phone book is the file in the database. Each file is composed of records, a single line in the phone book. Each record is composed of fields. Fields in the phone book would be the name, address, and phone number.

There are three major functions of a database management system — storage and maintenance, retrieval and query, and reporting.

Storage and Maintenance

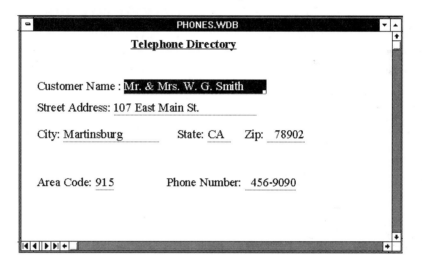

Data entry screen

The first function of a database management system is to allow you to enter the data and store it electronically. Most systems will allow you to create a data entry screen. The screen can look just like a normal printed form with areas for you to enter data for each field in a record. To move from one field to another, you press the tab key. Once you complete one form, the data is written to your database and stored as a record. You can then enter your next record.

Maintaining the data is another important function of the database. Maintaining the data means changing the data when the existing data becomes obsolete. For example, you must remove numbers from the phone book when phones are disconnected, add numbers when new phones are installed, and change addresses when people move. Database systems provide simple ways for you to perform these maintenance functions.

PHONES.WDB			
	Customer Name	Area Code	Phone Number
1	Mr. & Mrs. W. G. Smith	915	456-9090
2	Mr. Robert G. Cline	215	891-0022
3	Mr. J. C. Snead	703	568-7011
4	Mr. & Mrs. P. B. Langly	703	568-6524
5	Mr. R. T. Smith	703	568-4477
6	Mr. U. C. Hanks	804	662-9022
7	Miss. K. L. Jones	915	456-8956
8	Mrs. Y. T. Smith	915	456-0002
9	Clayton C. Roads	215	891-2222
10	Mrs. D. F. Street	703	568-9022
11	Mr. H. F. Smith	804	662-3379
12	Mrs. Q. A. Turner	915	456-0267
13	Miss. R. C. Jones	804	662-8910
14	Mr. P. B. Smith	915	456-7735
15	Wilson T. Jones	703	568-0202
16	J. P. Miller	915	456-2678
17	Dr. Paul T. Timple		
18	Robert L. Smith		

Database showing query

PHONES.WDB			
	Customer Name	Area Code	Phone Number
1	Mr. & Mrs. W. G. Smith	915	456-9090
5	Mr. R. T. Smith	703	568-4477
8	Mrs. Y. T. Smith	915	456-0002
11	Mr. H. F. Smith	804	662-3379
14	Mr. P. B. Smith	915	456-7735
18	Robert L. Smith	804	662-3191
19			
20			
21			
22			
23			

The next function of a database management system allows you to retrieve data. Each record in a database has a *key*. The key is data in a field that will make each record unique. For example, your social security number would make your record unique. To retrieve your record, you would enter your social security number, or other key, and request a retrieve operation. The software would search through the thousands of records that may be on the database and find your record.

When you *query* a database, you request a set of records based upon some criteria. Using the telephone book example again, you may want to locate all the people on a particular street. To find these, you would enter the street name. Other examples might be finding all students that are seniors or finding all books about a certain subject. Queries can be simple, like finding a record with a certain key, or they can be complex. Complex queries find records that have several characteristics. An example of a complex query would be to find all males over 21 years old who have an income between $15,000 and $20,000 and own a computer system that is over two years old, but who do not own more than one automobile that is more than three years old.

The last function of database management software is reporting. This software makes it easy to create sophisticated and complex reports in a relatively short time. In most systems, all you need to do is specify which fields you want to appear on a report. The database software sets up your headings and page numbers, formats the data into columns, and prints the report automatically. If you did not want to report all the data in the database, you could perform a query on the database before you print the report. Only those records found by the query would be reported.

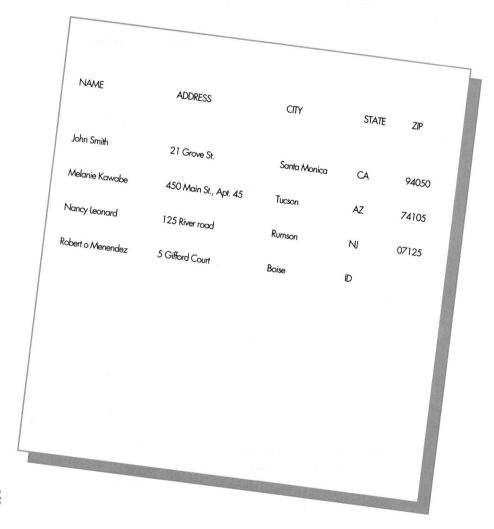

NAME	ADDRESS	CITY	STATE	ZIP
John Smith	21 Grove St.	Santa Monica	CA	94050
Melanie Kawabe	450 Main St., Apt. 45	Tucson	AZ	74105
Nancy Leonard	125 River road	Rumson	NJ	07125
Robert o Menendez	5 Gifford Court	Boise	ID	

Database report

Most database systems will also allow you to report statistics about the data. For example, you may want totals or subtotals of certain columns. You can also report the average of a column, the highest or lowest numbers, and many other statistics.

Using a word processing program and a database together, you can create a standard form letter in your word processing program and merge it with data from your database. Different fields from the database will be inserted into the form letter, and everyone on the database gets a personalized letter. Once the letters are printed, you can have the database print mailing labels for the letter or print on the envelopes themselves. This type of operation is called a *mail merge*.

Among the more popular database management systems are **dBase IV**, **Paradox**, **Fox Base**, and **R-Base**.

COMMON FEATURES OF DATABASE SOFTWARE

Data Entry Forms	Manual and Automatic Update
Data Formatting	Forms and List Views
Combine Multiple Databases	Sorting
Simple Query	Complex Queries (AND, OR, NOT)
Reporting	Statistics
Mail Merge	Mailing Labels
Combining Multiple Files	Backup

Graphics Software

Graphics software allows you to create, modify, display and print charts, pictures and designs. This type of software generally falls into three different categories — presentation graphics software, paint and draw software, and design software.

Presentation Graphics

The most common type of graphics software is used for presentation graphics. This type of graphics software is used to present comparisons of different data, like the increase or decrease in profits of a company or the comparison of voter preferences over a period of years. Once the data is graphed or charted, it can be

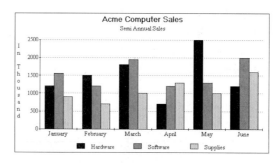

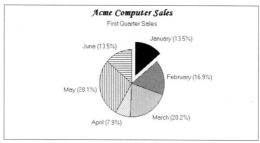

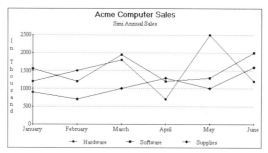

used in presentations, thus the term presentation graphics. These charts and graphs make it easier for an audience to get the big picture of the data without getting bogged down in the details of the numbers.

Simple presentation graphs consist of bar charts, line charts, and pie charts. Many electronic spreadsheet programs can produce these types of graphs. More sophisticated presentation graphics programs can produce three dimensional graphs and use picture images (called pictographs) to compare data rather than simple bars and lines.

Once the data for a graph has been entered and a graph has been created, you can change the type of graph simply by choosing a different graph type from a menu. Most presentation graphics programs allow you to define titles for the graph, choose different colors for different areas, determine what scale is used in the graph, and display *legends* on the graph. Popular presentation graphics programs include **Harvard Graphics** and **Perspective.**

Paint and Draw Graphics

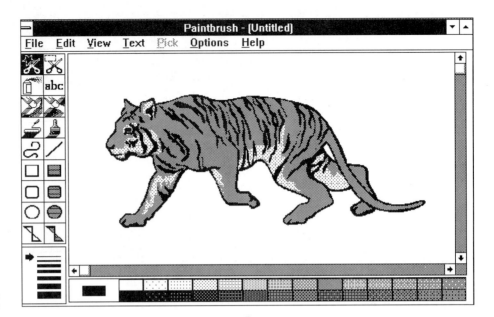

PC paint window

Paint and Draw graphics programs allow you to be an artist with your computer. Paint and draw programs provide you with tools such as a paint brush, spray can, pencil, and eraser, along with basic geometric shaping tools such as squares, circles, ovals, and lines. You perform your drawing and painting by selecting a tool and using a mouse, light pen, or some other input device to move the tools around on the screen. Using combinations of these tools, you can create pictures for catalog advertisements, business logos, invitations, newspaper ads, and numerous other things.

Once a picture is created, you can test different colors and shades in different areas of the picture with a single keystroke. You can also reduce or enlarge the entire drawing or any part of the drawing. You can move parts of a drawing from one position to another, duplicate parts, and erase parts with a simple keystroke or click of the mouse. You can also reshape an area by slanting it, bending it, or curving it. You can even take several different drawings and put them together to create scenes.

If you have little or no artistic talent, you can purchase thousands of images called *clip art images* from independent companies. With these images, you can use the painting and drawing software to design your own layouts and scenes. After you have created the images you want, you can insert them into your word processing or desktop publishing documents. Popular paint and draw graphics programs include **Aldus Freehand**®, **Adobe™ Illustrator**, **Mac Paint**, and **Mac Draw**.

Learn PC Computer Literacy

Design Graphics

Design software is used predominately by engineers and architects although they may also be used by chemists, biologists, and other professionals. This type of graphics software consists of many different symbols. Using a mouse, light pen or other input device, the designer selects different symbols and arranges then on the screen to produce an electronic schematic diagram, building blueprint, or other diagram.

Because different professions use different symbols and perform different types of work, design graphics software is tailored to a specific profession or discipline. For example, architectural software would have symbols of doors, windows, cabinets, and staircases; whereas electrical design software would have symbols of tubes, switches, and circuits.

Using an example of an architect, the architect can design a house for a buyer. If the buyer wants a wall or door moved, or a different type of window, the architect can make the change within seconds using a few simple keystrokes. Without the software, the architect would need to erase and redraw the blueprint, taking several hours instead of seconds. Popular design graphics programs include **Claris CAD**, **Blueprint**, and **Mac Draft**.

Telecommunication Software

Imagine using your computer from your home to pay your bills, check hotel rates in a different state, order tickets for a concert, check out a video tape, or learn about a new disease. With a *modem* and telecommunication software, you can do this.

Telecommunication software allows you to use your telephone line and your modem to communicate with other computers around the world. Once you have connected to the other computer system, you have access to its data. You can copy the data from the other computer back to yours (*download*), or you can send data to the other computer (*upload*)./send

Use of telecommunications is the fastest growing of all computer applications. In almost every city, computer users have set up electronic *bulletin board systems (BBS)*. Any computer user can connect to these bulletin boards and post notices for other users to read, read notices posted by other users, or upload and download data and software. Many companies have created bulletin boards of their own. These bulletin boards contain information on new products, sale prices, product recall information, technical help, and new product demonstrations. Popular communication programs include **Procomm Plus, Bitcom,** and **White Knight**.

Integrated Software

Application programs with each of the software categories discussed above can be purchased independently. When they are purchased independently, you get a sophisticated software program that is very powerful. Many software manufacturers have also developed integrated packages. An integrated package may contain all five types of software — word processing, spreadsheet, graphics, database, and telecommunications, or it may contain some combination of the five.

In an integrated package, each type of software will probably have fewer capabilities than they would if you purchased them separately, however, they will have everything a beginning user needs. Integrated packages can save you money because they are much cheaper than independent packages. In many cases you can get all five types of software for less than one independent package. A second advantage is that integrated packages are easier to learn. You only learn to use one package as opposed to five different packages.

Perhaps the greatest advantage of an integrated package is its ability to combine data from the different software types. For example, suppose you wanted to create a report in your word processing program that contained data and graphs from your spreadsheet. You also wanted to include information from the database. This is easy to do with an integrated package. If you were using an independent software program, it would be difficult at best, and it may not even be possible, depending upon the software used. Common integrated packages include **Microsoft® Works** and **Claris Works.**

Software Utilities

There are a number of software programs that fall somewhere between system software and application software. These programs are often called software utilities. Utility programs perform certain operations that are needed but are not included as part of the operating system or part of an application program. There are many of these utility programs available that perform an almost limitless number of tasks. The following figure lists some of the available utility programs and their functions.

COMMON TYPES OF UTILITY PROGRAMS

Alarm clocks:	Allows you to set alarms that remind you of different appointments, etc.
Backup utilities:	Creates and restores backup copies of disk files or disks.
Device drivers:	Allows different hardware devices to be used by your computer.
Diagnostic:	Checks your system hardware for possible problems and malfunctions.
Disk compression and reorganization:	Compression utilities force files to occupy less space on a disk. Reorganization utilities change the way files are stored on the disk to improve hard disk performance.
Disk tool kits:	Recovers data on and repairs damaged disks.
File converters:	Converts files created by one application program into a format that can be used by a different application program.
Menus:	Allows you to setup different commands so you can choose them from a menu rather than typing them.
Screen capture:	Takes a "picture" of your screen and stores it as a graphic image so it can be used in a paint or draw program.
Screen savers:	Blanks your screen when there is no keyboard activity after a specified time period. Saves the screen from being burned in.
Spoolers:	Allows your computer to print files at the same time you are working on the computer.
Virus detectors:	Detects common viruses in programs.
Virus vaccine:	Removes viruses from infected programs.

Now that you understand something about software, you need to know how to build a personal software library.   There are three different classes of software that you can use — *proprietary*, *shareware*, and *public domain* software.

Proprietary Software

SOFTWARE SYSTEMS COMPANY
End User License Agreement

PLEASE RETURN THE REGISTRATION FORM WHICH APPEARS I THE ENCLOSED USER'S MANUAL TO RECEIVE REGISTRATION BENEFITS.

BY OPENING THIS DISK ENVELOPE YOU ACCEPT ALL THE TERMS AND CONDITIONS OF THIS AGREEMENT. If you do not agree with the terms and conditions of this Agreement, return the disk envelope, UNOPENED, along with the rest of the package, immediately to Software Systems Company or the location where you obtained it.

This package contains application software and related Documentation. The application software and any upgrades are collectively referred to as the "Software." In return for acquiring a license to use the Software and Documentation, you agree to the following terms and conditions:

1. **Scope of Use.** (a) Application Software - You may use the application software on a single central processing unit. You may not use the application software on a multi-user unit.

2. **Assignment.** You may assign your rights under this Agreement to a third party who agrees in writing to be bound by this Agreement prior to the assignment provided that you transfer all copies of the Software and the Documentation in any form to the third party or destroy any copies not transferred. Except as set forth above, you may not assign your rights under this Agreement or loan, rent, lease, or transfer the Software. You agree that the Software will not be shipped, transferred, or exported into any country or used in any manner prohibited by the United States Export Administration Act.

3. **Proprietary Rights and Obligations.** The structure and organization of the Software are valuable trade secrets of Software Systems Company and its suppliers and we licensed to you on a non-exclusive basis. You agree to hold such trade secrets in confidence. You further agree not to translate, disassemble, decompile, or reverse engineer the Software, in whole or in part. You will not make or have made, or permit to be made, any copies of the Software, Documentation, or any part thereof, except one (1) copy solely for backup purposed or such copies as are necessary for installation of the Software in accordance with the terms of the is Agreement. Any such copies of the Software shall contain the same proprietary notices which appear on or in the Software. Trademarks shall be used in accordance with accepted trademark practice, including identification of trademark owner's name. Trademarks can only be used to identify printed output produced by the Software.

4. **No Other Rights.** Software Systems Company and its suppliers retain title and ownership of the Software, the media on which it is recorded, and all subsequent copies of the Software, regardless of the form or media in or on which the original and other copies may exist. Except as stated above, this Agreement does not grant you any rights to patents, copyrights, trade secrets, trademarks or any other rights in respect of the Software and Documentation. The use of any trademark does not give you any rights of ownership in that trademark.

5. **Term.** The license is effective until terminated. Software Systems Company has the right to terminate your license immediately if you fail to comply with any term of the Agreement. Upon any such termination, you must destroy the original and any copies of the Software and Documentation and cease all use of the trademarks.

A typical software
license agreement

Proprietary software is software that is always owned by the company that writes the software. When you purchase proprietary software, you only purchase the right to use the software, not the software itself. You cannot copy the software, except to make your own backup copy, and it is illegal to distribute the software to others. In fact, you do not even have the right to sell the software or manuals to someone else.

Buying proprietary software is the most common technique for obtaining software. The software is generally quite sophisticated and powerful and comes with good documentation and manuals. You can buy proprietary software from retail computer software stores and from mail order catalogs. Most retail computer stores will demonstrate the software and give you a chance to test it before you buy.

Shareware

The second type of software is *shareware*. With shareware you can use the software for a limited period of time. If you find the software useful and intend to continue using it, you are asked to register the software for a nominal fee, usually between $15 and $25. This registration gives you the right to continue to use the software. With shareware, you are asked to make copies of the software and distribute the copies to friends and colleagues; however, you cannot sell the copies or make a profit by distributing them.

Shareware is usually less sophisticated and more limited than proprietary software. Most shareware consists of games and utility programs; however, you can find word processing programs, spreadsheet, database, and other software in shareware libraries. The most common way of obtaining shareware is from electronic bulletin boards or from friends who have a copy of the software.

Public Domain Software

The third type of software is *public domain software*. This software is free. There is no limitation on the use of the software, and you are free to copy and distribute it. Public domain software is usually created by individuals rather than companies, and the creator simply wants to give it to other users. You can find the same types of software in the public domain libraries as you find in shareware libraries. You can obtain public domain software from electronic bulletin boards.

Software Compatibility

A computer can use, or RUN, an endless number and variety of software. Most software is written to run on a type of computer system rather than a particular computer system. For example, if software is written for an IBM-PC, the software will run on almost any IBM-PC or PC compatible computer as long as the computer has sufficient memory for the program.

There will be some exceptions to this rule. Sometimes the software must use a particular processor. For example, the software may require that the computer have a 286 or 386 processor. Some software may also require a particular graphics adapter. For example, the software may require that you have a EGA or VGA graphics adapter. Other software may require that you use a certain type or version of operating system.

You should also be aware that software written for Apple brand computers, such as the Apple II or Apple Macintosh, will not run on IBM-PC and PC compatible computers. There will be other cases where software will only run on certain brands of computers. Virtually all software specifies the processor type required, memory required, and a video adapter required. Make sure you check these requirements before buying software.

When you buy software, you need to make sure it is compatible with your computer system. There are also other things you should consider. First, check to make sure that no special additional hardware is required. Next, check the upgrade policy of the vendor. Software will be improved and new versions will be released. The upgrade policy states how you can receive new copies of the improved software. In some cases, the upgrade is free. In other cases, you must pay some reduced fee for the upgraded software. In still other cases, there is no upgrade policy, and you must pay full price for the upgrade. Check the company's policy before you buy.

You should also consider the manuals and other documentation provided with the software. Check it for readability and make sure it is written at your level of expertise. Check the index and table of contents to make sure operations are easy to find. Also, look for examples of how to do things.

CONSUMER TIPS BEFORE BUYING SOFTWARE

- What computer brand is the software written for?

- What is the minimum processor required (8086, 80286, 80386, 80486)?

- What is the minimum memory requirements (RAM)?

- Which graphics adapter is required?

- Which operating system is required?

- Is there additional hardware required (hard disk required, cables, cards.. etc)?

- What is the software maker's upgrade policy?

- Are there quality manuals and other documentation available?

- Is there good technical support?

Finally, check for technical support. No matter how knowledgeable you are or how well the manuals are written, there will be times when you need help. Most proprietary software vendors provide a toll free (800) number for technical support.

Computer Viruses

No discussion about software can be complete without some mention of computer viruses. A computer virus is a set of instructions that is designed to damage your computer hardware, software, and data, or interfere with the proper operation of your computer system in some way. Some viruses attack your software and make it behave erratically. Other viruses attack your data and may destroy files or erase entire disks. These programs are developed by unscrupulous people who take joy in the misery of others.

Computer viruses work like human viruses. They attach themselves to one program. Then, when the infected program is run, the virus will attach to another program. Before you know it, all of your programs are infected. Eventually, the virus will begin doing its damage. You may turn your computer on some morning and find that all of your software and data have been erased.

Most viruses come from electronic bulletin boards, but they may come from any program. In many cases they are unknowingly passed from user to user through shareware or public domain software. A friend may unknowingly infect your system, simply by using his or her program on your computer. There have even been cases where viruses were attached to proprietary software during the production of the software.

The best way to protect yourself from a virus is with a virus detection program. These programs scan a hard disk or diskette each time the disk is used, looking for signs of common viruses. Be aware that virus detectors are not foolproof. New viruses are constantly being developed of which your virus detector may not be aware. You will need to upgrade your virus detection program constantly so that it can detect newer viruses. You can also get *virus vaccines*. A vaccine is a program that removes the virus from your files.

SOME SIGNS OF A COMPUTER VIRUS

- Your computer system begins to act erratically.

- Programs begin to quit abnormally, for no known reason.

- You begin to run out of memory when you know you should have free memory available.

- Your computer begins to slow down as if it were getting tired.

- Files begin to get larger for no known reason.

- Files begin to disappear.

- New files begin to appear on your hard disk.

- Files get moved from one location to another.

It is important to keep backup copies of your data and programs. If your system does get infected, your vaccine may not be able to remove the virus. If this happens, you may need to destroy your original files and restore them from the backup. Be aware that your backup files may also be infected so they need to be checked for an infection before restoring them.

Some common virus detectors and vaccines are **Virex-PC, Disinfectant, SAM,** and **Virus Detective.**

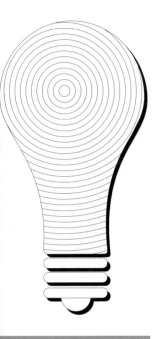

Summary

- Application software allows a user to accomplish a job-related task. The most common applications software are word processing, electronic spreadsheets, and database, graphics, and telecommunications.

- Word processing software allows you to create, revise, format, store, and print documents. Word processing software is used when the majority of your work involves words and text.

- Desktop publishing software is similar to word processing software but desktop publishing software gives you more capabilities to include graphic images in your documents.

- Electronic spreadsheet software is used when you deal primarily with numbers. Spreadsheets allow you to enter your numbers in cells then perform calculations based upon the numbers you enter.

- Database software is used when you need to keep records about people, places, or things. Database software has three general functions: creation and maintenance; retrieval and query; and reporting functions.

- Graphics software allows you to create charts, pictures, or designs. Graphics software categories are presentation, paint and draw, and design graphics.

- Telecommunications software allows you to use a modem to communicate with other computer systems and electronic bulletin boards.

- Many software programs combine several applications areas into a single program. These programs are called integrated programs.

- There are three kinds of software — proprietary, shareware, and public domain software.

- A computer virus is a program that damages your software and data. A virus spreads from one system to another by attaching itself to other software when a contaminated program is run. Virus detectors warn you of a possible virus. Virus vaccines remove a virus from a program.

Review Questions

Answer the following questions to check your understanding of the lesson material.

1. How does application software differ from system software?

2. Distinguish between system software and application software.

3. Explain what a cut and paste operation is.

4. What does the term WYSIWYG mean?

5. Data in an electronic spreadsheet are stored in areas called_____. Each one of these storage areas is identified by a _____ letter and a _____number.

6. What is the difference between a spreadsheet function and a spreadsheet macro?

7. List the three major database functions and explain what each does.

8. List the three categories of graphics software and explain how they differ.

9. List several different functions a utility program might perform.

10. Describe three different ways you can obtain software.

11. Discuss several questions you should ask before buying software.

12. What are computer viruses? How do they spread? How do you prevent them?

Glossary

101 key keyboard Standard microcomputer keyboard. It has one hundred and one keys including a numeric keypad, 12 function keys, and cursor movement keys

68020 32 bit chip used in the Macintosh LC and Classic computers.

68030 32 bit high performance CPU chip used in the Macintosh SI computer.

68040 Fastest Motorola 32 bit chip used in Macintosh Quadra computers.

80286 An enhanced 16 bit CPU that forms the entry level for current microcomputers and comes with the ISA bus.

80386 DX A 32 bit CPU available with any bus system. Provides excellent performance and is the preferred CPU for average personal use.

80386 SX A 32 bit CPU coupled with a 16 bit bus so performance is slower than the 80386 DX chip but much faster than the 80286 CPU.

80486 DX An extremely powerful 32 bit CPU chip available for all bus systems. Appropriate for the most demanding processing requirements. Comes with a special math coprocessor unit that enhances mathematical processing.

80486 SX The same 32 bit processor as the 80486 DX but without the math coprocessor and, therefore, somewhat less expensive.

8088 16 bit CPU chip used in the original IBM PC and clones. Too slow for most current software.

Add-on Board See Expansion Card.

Analog communication A method of communication in which tones or frequencies are sent over phone lines. Voice communication is a good example of analog transmission.

Apple Macintosh	Developed by the Apple Corporation, a family of personal computers that is easy to use and powerful.
Applications software	A program or set of programs used to perform specific job related tasks. Examples are word processors, electronic spreadsheets, database management systems, and graphics programs.
Arithmetic Logic Unit	A component of the central processing unit that performs all arithmetic (addition, subtraction, multiplication, and division) and logical comparisons between numbers.
ASCII	Abbreviation for American Standard Code for Information Interchange which is a binary code defining the binary representation for each letter, number, and symbol.
Auto park heads	Read/write heads on a hard or fixed disk that automatically withdraw from the disk drive when the power is turned off.
Auto-repeat keys	Characteristic of most computer keyboard keys. When the key is held down for several seconds, the key begins repeating as long as it is held down. This is like pressing the key several times.
Backup	A duplicate copy of data. The backup is made so that you have a copy of the data in case the original data is lost, destroyed, or damaged.
Bar Code Scanner	Input device used to interpret bar codes. The scanner examines the width and distance between the bars to assign a numeric code. Bar code scanners can be of the hand held or flat bed style.
Binary digit (bit)	A 1 or 0 in the binary representation. Used in groups to form a byte.
Bits per second (bps)	A measure of speed when transmitting digital data over communications lines. Also a measure of the speed of a modem with common speeds being 300, 1200, 2400, 4800 and 9600 bits per second.
Bus LAN	A local area network that has one main wire or bus to which all computers are connected.
Bus	See Data bus.
Byte	A group (usually 8 in personal computers) of bits that form a character.
Cache memory	Special random access memory that is used to speed up transfer of data from secondary storage devices and the CPU.
Cathode Ray Tube	The TV-like picture tube in the computer monitor. Also called the CRT.
CGA (Color Graphics Adapter)	A card that enables a computer to output both color and graphics. This adapter card provides 4 colors and a resolution of 320 by 200 pixels on the screen.

CD-ROM	Compact Disk Read Only Memory — A type of direct access optical storage media. CD-ROM is a read-only media with large storage capacity.
Central Processing Unit	An electronic circuit chip found inside the system unit that does the processing of information. Also called a microprocessor.
Clip art	Computer images or pictures used in desk top publishing applications to help illustrate or enhance an article or brochure.
Clipboard	An area in memory where data can be stored and later inserted into other application programs.
Clock speed	The speed at which the central processing unit can process instructions. Measured in MHz.
Clones	A common name given to personal computers that function like the IBM line of personal computers but are built by other manufacturers.
Color graphics adapter card	Card inserted into a slot in the system unit. Color graphic adapter cards enable a computer to output color and graphic characters. See CGA, EGA, VGA, SVGA and XGA.
Compiler	Translates a high level English like computer language into a low level, machine language.
Compuserve	A commercial information service that offers a wide variety of features. To use the service, you subscribe by paying a low monthly fee.
Computer literacy	The process of learning enough about the computer to be both a knowledgeable user and purchaser of computers.
Computer privacy	See Privacy.
Computer viruses	See Viruses.
Control Unit	A component of the central processing unit that controls all processing operations.
CPU	See Central Processing Unit.
CRT	See Cathode Ray Tube.
Cursor	Small flashing symbol on a computer screen. The symbol may be an underscore, block, cross hair, or an arrow. The cursor indicates where typing will occur.
Data	Unprocessed facts that have been input into the computer such as numbers or letters typed from the keyboard.
Database	A file or group of files composed of fields and records that contain information about people, places, or things.
Database software	Often called Database Management Systems (DBMS), allow you to store, edit, retrieve, and generate reports from data on an electronic database.

Data bus	An electronic highway located on the motherboard that connects the CPU with all other devices installed in the computer. See ISA, EISA, and MCA.
Data call	A telephone connection or call between two computers.
Data communications	The general name given to computer communications.
Data Density	A measure of how close together the bits on a storage media are placed. The data density helps determine the total data capacity of the media.
Demodulate	The changing of analog signals into a digital format by a modem.
Desktop computer	Classic personal computer where the system unit cabinet forms a base for the monitor and sits on the desktop. It is easy to expand using expansion cards.
Design Graphics	Graphics software that allows you to select pre-drawn symbols to create electronic schematic layouts, blue prints, and engineering designs.
Device drivers	Software programs that aid input and output devices in the interpretation of data. Each input and output device must have a special driver that helps it communicate with the processor.
Digital	Information that is represented by a 1 or a 0 using binary digits or bits.
Direct access device	Normally a disk drive. Direct access devices allow the read/write heads to move to the required data without reading the data in sequence.
Disk drive	A device that can read or write information on a magnetic disk. These disks can be removable (see Diskette) or stationary (see fixed disk).
Diskette	A removable magnetically coated disk onto which the computer can read or write data with the disk drive. Available in plastic covered 3.5" and floppy 5.25" sizes.
Dot Matrix Printers	An inexpensive printer that uses a combination of dots to print letters or symbols on a page. This printer prints one character at a time and is noisy in operation.
Downloading	Moving information from a host or central computer to your computer over communication lines.
Draw graphics	Similar to paint graphics, these software programs allow you to create pictures and artwork.
Drawing pad	Touch input device used to input hand drawn images into the computer. This device uses a special pen and drawing pad. As you draw on the pad, the image is transferred into memory.
EGA (Enhanced Graphics Adapter)	A card that enables a computer to output both color and graphics. This adapter card provides 16 colors and a resolution of 640 by 350 pixels on the screen.
EISA data bus	See Enhanced Industry Standard Architecture.

Electroluminescent Display	Flat screen display technology that uses a grid of small wires embedded in a specially treated material that glows in response to electricity. Each point where two wires cross forms a pixel.
Electronic bulletin board	A system that is shared by multiple computer users. Allows a user to post and receive messages and to upload and download other files.
Electronic cottage	Term describing people that can work at home yet communicate with their office through the use of a computer.
Enhanced Industry Standard Architecture	32 bit data bus that is compatible with the very common Industry Standard Architecture (ISA) expansion cards. Needed for very demanding processing tasks such as network control computers.
Erasable optical disk	Diskette media that stores data using optical technology. Unlike CD-ROM and WORM technology, these disks can be erased and written.
Expansion cards	Electronic circuit boards that can be plugged into expansion slots on the motherboard. These allow for the computer to be upgraded quickly.
Expansion slots	Special receptacles connected to the data bus that receive expansion cards. Each type of data bus (ISA, EISA, and MCA) has different expansion slot requirements but EISA can use the older ISA expansion cards.
External modem	Self contained modem that is installed outside the system unit and connected to the computer's serial port.
Field	A string of characters that, when taken as a single unit, provide some meaning to an object stored. Fields are the components of records.
File server	A large personal computer that is used to store programs and data for many users on a local area network.
File	A set of records that contain like data. Files are normally the unit of data that is stored in a particular area of the disk.
Film recorder	Output device that stores output on a 35 mm filmstrip.
Fixed disks	See Hard disk.
Floppy disk	A 5 1/4 inch removable magnetic disk storage media. Floppy disks are direct access media and are used to store data.
Font	Fonts are character shapes or character styles. Many printers allow you to print output using different fonts and font sizes.
Formatting	The process of preparing a disk to store data. The formatting process defines the tracks and cylinders on disk and determines the data density. Formatting is performed by software.

Function keys	A set of special keys, labeled F1, F2 ...F12 on the computer keyboard. Each key performs a special operation. The operation performed depends upon the software program being used.
Gas Plasma Display	A flat screen display technology that uses a gas trapped between two panes of glass. Gas plasma screens produce a sharper, brighter display than LCD screens and do not flicker like cathode ray tubes.
Genie	Commercial information service, offered by the General Electric Company, that is connected to with your personal computer and a modem.
GIGO	Term that stands for Garbage In—Garbage Out. This term implies that the output from the computer can not be better or more accurate than the input to the computer.
Grammar checker	Computer software that checks writing for proper English syntax rules. They normally suggest the reason a sentence is not grammatically correct and offer possible corrective action. Usually part of a word processor.
Hard copy	Printed output. Printers produce a hard copy output because the output can be touched. Compare this to soft copy.
Hard disk	Hard disks that are permanently mounted in the disk drive. Fixed disks are not removable. Fixed disks provide higher storage capacity and faster access than floppy disks.
Hardware	A general term given to all physical components of the computer. Hardware can be seen and touched.
Hayes compatible	Modem specification that makes it easier to connect to other computers. Your modem should be Hayes compatible.
Head crash	A type of hardware failure on disk drives. When a head crash occurs, the disk's read/write heads touch the disk. This error normally renders the disk unusable.
IBM/PC	IBM's family of computers also called the IBM/Personal Computer and the IBM PS/2
Image Scanners	Input devices that use optical technology to convert printed images into computer input data. Most image scanners can convert both pictures and characters.
Industry Standard Architecture	A 16 bit data bus standard that is the most common in personal computers. Suitable for most single user requirements. Operates slower than EISA or MCA.
Information	Data that has been processed by the computer and then stored as information.
Ink jet printer	A non-impact printer technology that sprays ink droplets on paper to form characters. Ink Jet printers produce a NLQ (near letter quality) image.
Input	The act of putting data into the computer in preparation for processing.

Integrated software	Application software that includes more than one function in a single program. An integrated package may include a word processor, electronic spreadsheet, and a graphics routine.
Intel CPU chip	Central processor chip made by the Intel Corporation. See also 8088, 80286, 80386 and 80486.
Internal modem	Modem that is installed inside the system unit by plugging into an expansion slot.
Interpreter	Performs the same job as a compiler; translates high level English language into machine language.
ISA data bus	See Industry Standard Architecture.
K bytes	Unit of measurement for memory that means approximately 1,000 characters or bytes. Actually, one K = 1,024 bytes but most users round down to 1,000.
Keyboard	The most common computer input device. This device inputs data by touch. It looks and acts much the same as a standard typewriter.
LAN	See Local Area Network.
Laptop computer	Small, portable unit which weighs 10 pounds or less. Usually more expensive than other microcomputers and harder to upgrade.
Laser printer	A non-impact printer technology that uses a laser beam directed at an imaging drum. The image is then transferred from the drum to the paper using a carbon toner. Laser printers produce a NTQ (near typeset quality) image.
Liquid Crystal Display (LCD)	A flat screen display technology that uses two thin layers of glass with a liquid chemical trapped between them. When the cells of the chemical darken, a character or image is formed. Major advantages of an LCD display are light weight and low power consumption.
Local Area Network	A network or group of connected personal computers that are in close proximity. Computers are connected with cables and do not require modems.
Macintosh computers	A family of personal computers, developed by the Apple Corporation, that is easy to use and powerful. The Macintosh is based on the Motorola CPU chip series.
Macro	Small program written in an application program that performs several steps with a single keystroke.
Magnetic Ink Character Recognition (MICR)	Input data coding technique that uses magnetic particles embedded in printing ink. The data is read by recognizing the image formed by the magnetic particles. This technique is used predominately by banks for tracking checks.

Mainframe computer	Very large, powerful business computer that can serve hundreds of users at a time. Used by large companies, these computers can cost millions of dollars.
Mark readers	Optical input device that recognizes pencil marks on coded forms. The graphite in the pencil lead is detected by reflected light. Used when very low volume input is required, like test scoring sheets.
Math coprocessor	An added processing unit, like a second CPU, that is optimized for mathematical processing functions. Very helpful for processing computerized design and drafting applications and desktop publishing.
MCA data bus	See Micro Channel Architecture.
Megabyte	One million bytes or characters are equal to one megabyte. Used when describing primary or secondary storage such as a disk.
Megahertz (MHz)	One million cycles per second. Used when describing the clock or processing speed of computers.
Memory	Primary storage of the computer, usually in the form of Random Access Memory (RAM) and Read Only Memory (ROM).
Micro Channel Architecture (MCA)	An IBM 32 bit data bus design that is not compatible with the ISA or EISA designs meaning those expansion cards will not fit the MCA system. Offers ease of use and excellent performance.
Microdisk	A 3 1/2 inch removable magnetic disk storage media. Micro disks are direct access media and are used to store data.
Microcomputer	A small, personal computer designed for one user. Can come in a desktop or laptop models and are powerful yet inexpensive. The most common computer available. Also called personal computers.
Microprocessor	An electronic chip that performs the processing in a computer and usually numbered to indicate relative performance with higher numbers being more powerful. See Central Processing Unit.
Minicomputer	A midrange computer that falls between a microcomputer and mainframe in size and cost.
MODEM	Device that coverts digital signals from a computer into analog sounds that can be transmitted over phone lines and vice versa. Must be used in pairs. MODEM is an abbreviation for MOdulate/DEModulate.
Modulate	The process of converting digital bits into analog sounds.
Monitor	The most common soft copy output display device found on microcomputers. Monitors normally use cathode ray technology.

Monochrome monitor	Term used to describe a monitor type. Monochrome monitors normally display only two colors — black and white, green and white, or amber and white. Some Monochrome monitors also display shades of gray.
Motherboard	The main electronic circuit board in the system unit of the computer. The motherboard holds the CPU chip, data bus, expansion cards, and provides connections to other devices.
Motorola CPU chip	CPU chip, designed by the Motorola Company, that is used in Macintosh computers.
Mouse	Touch input device that is used to move the cursor on the computer screen or to select options from a software menu. Mice can be either mechanical or optical guided devices.
MS-DOS	Microsoft-Disk Operating System. Operating system commonly found on IBM-PC compatible microcomputers.
Multitasking	Allows a computer to run several programs at the same time.
Music synthesizer	An audio input and output device that takes sound waves and stores them electronically in the computer. Music synthesizers can both input and output sound.
Network	Several computers connected together by wires or telephone lines so that users may share information and programs.
Nodes	Computers on a Local Area Network that are not file servers.
Numeric keypad	A set of 17 keys set apart from the character keys on a computer keyboard. The keys include all 10 digits of the decimal numbering systems along with the keys for arithmetic operations (+,-,/,*, decimal point, and an enter key).
Operating system	Set of software programs that control the hardware of a computer system. Performs such tasks as managing memory, directing input and output operations, checking for and displaying errors, etc.
Output	Information that has been processed by the computer and printed or displayed on the screen or other device that moves information out of the computer.
Paint graphics	Software that provides tools like paint brushes, spray cans, pencils, and geometric shapes so you can create drawings and artwork.
Parallel port	Plug connected to the motherboard that allows a device (usually a printer) to be plugged into the computer. Sends eight bits (one byte) at a time.
PC-DOS	Same as MS-DOS but written for IBM brand computers.
Pen plotters	A type of graphic hard copy output device. These devices use color pens to draw graphs and artwork. The two types of pen plotters are flat bed and drum.

Pen-based writing pad	Touch input device that uses a special pen and pad to input handwriting into the computer. The writing on the pad is interpreted by the computer software and stored as if it had been typed on the keyboard.
Personal computer	See microcomputer.
Pictographs	A type of chart that uses symbols or pictures to graphically compare of data.
Pixel	A pixel is a picture element or point of light on a display screen. Combinations of lighted pixels are used to display characters and images on a screen. The numbers of pixels on a screen determine a screen's resolution.
Point	1/72nd of an inch. Used to define the height of a character or font.
Port	A plug, usually on the back of the system cabinet, used to attach input and output devices to the computer system. Ports can be either serial or parallel.
Postscript	A language used for creating drawings and artwork. Postscript images provide sharper, clearer images when they are enlarged or reduced.
Presentation graphics	Software that allows you to generate charts from numbers. Charts are typically bar, pie, and line types but may also be pictographs.
Primary storage	Storage for information used by the CPU for processing that uses special electronic chips to hold the information. This storage is erased when the power to the computer is turned off. See also Memory.
Printer	A mechanical device that causes output from the computer to be printed on a page of paper. Printers are available in several types see dot matrix, ink jet, and laser printers.
Privacy	Responsible computer users have to ensure that data they access are not divulged to unauthorized users.
Processing	Transforming of data into desired information by the computer.
Prodigy	Popular commercial information service that offers many different types of data including sports scores, news, and airline reservations.
Program	A series of computer instructions that tell the computer exactly how to perform some specific task.
Proprietary software	Software that is always owned by the corporation that developed it. Propriety software cannot be copied, or sold.
Proportional printer	A printer characteristic that uses a different amount of horizontal space for each character printed, depending upon the actual amount of space required by the character.
Public domain software	Software that is free. You can copy and use the software free of charge.

Query
A request for certain information based upon some set of given criteria. For example, you may query a database to list all seniors that are graduating and have red hair.

Qwerty keyboard
Standard key layout for computer keyboards and typewriters. The Qwerty key layout determines the location of the different keys on the keyboard. Named for the first six keys of the top left portion of the letters of the keyboard.

Random Access Memory (RAM)
Electronic chips that store information and programs that are used by the CPU. This memory is volatile in that memory contents are erased when the computer power is turned off.

Read Only Memory (ROM)
Memory holding permanent information used by the system that was placed on the chip when it was constructed. ROM is nonvolatile so it can never be erased or written to by the user.

Read/write head
The recording device for storage devices. These heads can both read the data from the media and write data to the media.

Record
A set of related data items (fields) about a particular object stored. Records are composed of fields. A collection of like records is a file.

Resolution
Clarity of an image. With monitors and display screens, resolution is determined by the number of pixels on the screen. With printers, resolution is determined by dots per inch.

Ring LAN
A local area network that is designed in a circular ring pattern. Offers excellent performance but at a higher cost than the bus or star LANs.

Screen image projectors
A soft copy output device that projects the images generated by a computer onto a wide screen, much like a slide projector. Screen image projectors require an overhead projector to display the image.

Secondary storage
Permanent storage of information that will not be lost when the computer is turned off. Usually in the form of disks or diskettes.

Sector
Part of a track on a disk. Each track is divided into several sectors. The sector gives the read/write heads a location point for the stored data.

Sequential access device
Magnetic tape storage. Sequential access devices must read each piece of data, one after another. They cannot move directly to the data they need.

Serial port
Receptacle connected to the motherboard that allows serial devices (normally the mouse or modem) to be connected to the computer. Sends information one bit at a time.

Shareware
Software that you can obtain from bulletin boards. You have permission to use the software for a limited period before you must pay a registration fee.

Site license	A license purchased from a software vendor that allows the use of the software program throughout the organization without the payment of added fees.
Soft copy	Computer output that cannot be touched. Computer monitors produce soft copy output.
Software	Programs that are written to tell the computer how to process data. Software is usually stored on secondary storage. You cannot physically touch software.
Software license	The right to use a given software program. Licenses are usually purchased from the firm that writes the program.
Software piracy	Illegally using software programs without paying for the program license.
Spell checker	A software routine normally found in word processors that checks the spelling of each word in a document against a dictionary. Spell checkers usually provide suggested spellings for a word that is spelled incorrectly.
Spreadsheet software	Software that allows you to enter numbers and text into columns and rows. Once the data is stored you can create formulas that are recalculated when any data is changed.
Storage	A place where the computer can store information and data when it is not being processed. See also Primary storage and Secondary storage.
Supercomputer	The most powerful, largest computers available. These are used for very complex problems in Government and research.
Syntax	Stands for the sentence structure of a statement. Commands in DOS and in programming language must conform to a precise sentence structure.
System software	The programs that direct and control the operation of a computer system.
System unit	The central box or cabinet of a microcomputer that houses the Central Processing Unit and the disk drives. The monitor, keyboard, and printer will connect to the system unit.
Star LAN	A local area network in which the file server is located in the center, and nodes radiate outward in a star pattern.
SVGA (super video graphics array)	A card that enables a computer to output both color and graphics. This adapter card provides 32,676 colors and a 768 by 1024 pixel resolution.
System unit	The cabinet that contains most of the computer's electronics including the motherboard, CPU, expansion slots, and disk drives.
Telecommunications	Communicating between computers using telephone lines and modems.
Telecommunications software	Programs that allow two or more computers to communicate; typically over telephone lines with a modem.

Template	Small diagram of the keys on the keyboard and the function of each key. Templates are normally made of cardboard or plastic and are different for each software program.
Thesaurus	Part of a word processing program that will offer different alternative words (synonyms) for a given word in a document.
Touch screen	Touch input device used to indicate a selection from a computer screen. Most touch screens are pressure sensitive. Several items are displayed on the screen, and you make a selection by touching the point on the screen where the item appears.
Tower computer	The system unit is arranged in a vertical position and sits on the floor next to the desk. Provides more space on the desk than the desktop and retains ease of expansion.
Trackball	Touch input device that looks like a mouse turned upside down. Performs the same functions as a mouse.
Track	An imaginary concentric circle on a disk. Tracks are used to store data. Tracks are defined when the disk is formatted.
Universal Product Code (UPC)	A standard bar code used on almost all packaged products. The code indicates the type of merchandise, the manufacturer's identification code, and the manufacturer's product code.
UNIX	An operating system that provides multitasking and is available for both mainframe and smaller computer systems.
Upgrade	(noun) An improved version of a computer program. (verb) To change from an older version of a program to a newer version.
Uploading	Transferring computer information to a host computer when using telecommunications.
Utility program	Software that performs a single basic function, like formatting a diskette or blanking a screen.
VDT	Video Display Terminal. See Video monitor.
VGA (video graphics array)	A card that enables a computer to output both color and graphics. This adapter card provides 256 colors and a 640 by 480 pixel resolution.
Version	The sequence number of a particular computer program. As programs are improved the version number increases with higher numbers indicating the more recent program.
Video monitor	The TV-like display of the computer. Monitors are available in color or monochrome versions.

Virtual memory	Memory that is actually auxiliary storage on a disk but is treated as if it is RAM memory. Using virtually memory effectively increases the amount of RAM available.
Virus	A software program written to damage or destroy program, data, or hardware. Viruses attach themselves to one program then infect other programs when the infected program is run.
Virus detector	Software program that checks other programs for the presence of a known virus.
Virus vaccine	Program that removes viruses from an infected program.
Voice call	Normal telephone call between two people.
Voice recognition	Technique where an input device listens to human speech and converts the speech into digital signals that can be stored in the computer.
Volatile memory	Memory that is erased when the computer is turned off.
Word processing software	Computer programs that allow you to create, edit, store, and print documents composed primarily of words.
WORM Write Once, Read Many optical disk	This type of optical disk can be written to only once. Once data has been stored on an area of the disk, that area becomes a read-only area.
Write-protect notch	A small notch in a 5 1/4 inch floppy disk. When the notch is covered with a small piece of tape, the disk cannot be erased or written to.
Write-protect switch	A small switch in the lower corner of a 3 1/2 inch micro disk. When this switch is in the down position, the disk cannot be erased or written to.
WYSIWYG	Abbreviation for *What You See Is What You Get*. Most often found in word processors. This means your computer screen will display a document exactly the same way it will be printed out.

Answers to Odd-Numbered Questions

Lesson 1

1. **Who uses computers today?**
   ANSWER: Just about everyone uses or is affected by computers. This trend will continue in the future.

3. **What are three important reasons for you to become computer literate?**
   ANSWER: Your employer will expect it; be able to purchase the correct computer for your home or office, use the computer to learn about other subjects, and to be prepared for the future.

5. **The three fundamental processing steps all computers utilize are:**
   ANSWER: All computers use the steps of Inputting, Processing and Outputting of information.

7. **What is the system unit?**
   ANSWER: The system unit is the main cabinet of the computer that houses the central processing unit, disk drives, and provides connections for the keyboard and monitor.

9. **How does telecommuting work?**
   ANSWER: Telecommuting allows an individual to connect his or her computer at home to the main computer in the office though the use of a modem and telephone line. The employee can then work "at the office" from their home, saving time and money usually spent commuting.

11. **What is a computer virus and how should you protect your computer from them?**

ANSWER: A virus is a program that infects your computer and can cause it to lose data. Protect the computer from virus infections by not sharing disks with others and using a virus detection program.

Lesson 2

1. **What is the function of an input device?**

ANSWER: The function of any input device is to convert data found in the outside world into an electronic form that can be understood by the computer.

3. **What does a device driver do?**

ANSWER: A device driver is a software program that tells hardware devices precisely how to perform their job. The are required for all hardware devices.

5. **Explain what a mouse is used for.**

ANSWER: The mouse is used as a pointing and selecting device rather than a data entry device. This means that you do not use the mouse to enter data; you use it to position the cursor or to select existing data and options from program menus.?

7. **List four different types of visual input devices and explain what kind of input each device can recognize.**

ANSWER: 1) Scanners; recognize pictures and text, 2) Bar-code reader; recognizes a bar code like the Universal Product Code, 3) Optical-mark reader; recognizes the presence or absence of a pencil mark, 4) Magnetic Ink Character Reader (MICR); recognizes the account numbers and amount on checks.

9. **Explain five different problems involved in voice recognition.**

ANSWER: 1)Voice inflection: Different people emphasize different sounds or syllables for emphasis which causes problems for the computer system. 2) Voice tone and voice changes: Some people have high voices and others have deep voices. The computer system must be able to interpret the different pitches of these voices. Also, when you have a cold or a sore throat, your voice changes. 3) Local accents: The accent of someone from Brooklyn, NY is dramatically different than someone from New Orleans, LA. 4) Localized words and slang words: For the system to work well, the words must be stored in a dictionary. This means that the dictionary must be updated constantly with local terms, slang words, and new words. 5) External noise, such as radios, background conversation, noisy machinery, etc., may be interpreted as speech.

Lesson 3

1. The "computer on a chip" located on the motherboard is called the
    _____.
    ANSWER: Central Processing Unit or CPU

3. **What does ALU stand for and what does it do?**
    ANSWER: Arithmetic Logic Unit. The ALU does all mathematical calculations and comparisons. It is part of the CPU.

5. **How are bits combined to represent a byte?**
    ANSWER: Each bit can represent a 1 or 0. Several (often 8) bits used together can represent one character or byte. These bit patterns are determined by the ASCII or EBCDIC bit codes.

7. **Why is RAM said to be volatile?**
    ANSWER: RAM is volatile since it will be erased when the power to the computer is turned off.

9. **To install a new color monitor, you will likely need to add a(n)**
    _____ **card into a(n)** _____ **slot on the motherboard.**
    ANSWER: expansion or add-on; expansion

11. **What is the difference between a serial and parallel port?**
    ANSWER: A serial port transmits data one bit at a time while the parallel port transmits data several bits (one byte) at a time.

Lesson 4

1. **What is the function of an output device?**
    ANSWER: The function of an output device is to present the data, that is stored in memory, to the user in a form that the user can understand. ?

3. **Give five characteristics of a computer monitor.**
    ANSWER: Size, Monochrome or Color, Resolution, ~~Resolution~~, Graphics Adapter required, Display Technology.

5. **How does the technology of a cathode ray tube monitor differ from the technology of a flat screen display?**
    ANSWER: Cathode ray tubes use a phosphorus coating on the screen. A beam is fired at the screen to make the pixel areas on the screen glow. Flat screens do not use phosphorus and do not use the gun. They either use liquid crystal, electroluminescent (wires), or gas.

7. The quality of printer material is determined by the number of _____ used to print the character.

ANSWER: Dots per inch (DPI).

9. **List three types of microcomputer printers and explain how each type produces its output.**

ANSWER: 1) Dot matrix; uses a series of pin and forms its image by. To form a character, a small hammer strikes certain pins that in turn strike an inked ribbon. 2) Ink jet; To print a character or image, the print head sprays droplets of ink onto the paper. 3) Laser printer; A laser beam is directed at a light sensitive printing drum. The laser beam forms an image of dots on the printing drum. This drum then places electrostatic charges on the paper. Next, a toner is deposited on the paper in the charged areas.

11. **How does a flatbed plotter differ from a drum plotter?**

ANSWER: On a flatbed plotter, two pens are dragged across the paper to draw an image. The paper does not move. On a drum printer, the paper is attached to a cylinder and the cylinder drags the paper beneath the pins.

Lesson 5

1. **List the six building blocks of data in order from smallest to largest.**

ANSWER: Bit, byte or character, field, record, file, database.

3. **What capability of a disk drive allows the drive to directly access the data?**

ANSWER: The capability to move the read/write heads to and track on the disk.

5. **What determines the data density of a diskette?**

ANSWER: The data density is determined by the hardware device (disk drive) and the software that formats the diskette.

7. **List two advantages of a hard or fixed disk.**

ANSWER: 1) larger storage capacity (20 to over 500 million bytes) and speed.

9. **List two advantages that optical storage has over magnetic storage.**

ANSWER: Stores a larger amount of data in the same amount of space and are not affected by magnetic fields and other environmental contaminates.

Lesson 6

1. **What kind of signal does the computer understand?]**
   ANSWER: The computer can only interpret digital signals made up of bits and bytes.

3. **What does the word MODEM stand for?**
   ANSWER: MODEM is short for MOdulate/DEModulate.

5. **Where does an external modem connect to the computer?**
   ANSWER: The external modem is connected to the serial port of the computer.

7. **If you wanted to receive an information file from a host computer, you would _____ it.**
   ANSWER: You will download from the host.

9. **Name the three most common LAN designs:**
   ANSWER: Bus, Star, Ring

Lesson 7

1. **Define the term software.**
   ANSWER: Computer software is a program, or set of programs, that tell the computer hardware (input, processor, output, and storage devices) how to perform certain tasks. A computer program is a detailed set of instructions that tell the computer the precise sequence of steps that must be taken to perform a task..

3. **Programmers write instructions in an English-like language that is converted to a machine language by a _____ or an _____.**
   ANSWER: Compiler, interpreter

5. **How do PC and MS-DOS differ from OS/2?**
   ANSWER: PC and MS-DOS are command oriented meaning that you normally type commands to tell them what you want performed. OS/2 is graphics oriented meaning that commands are used by selecting icons or menu options.

7. **Microsoft Windows is not an operating system. What is it?**
   ANSWER: Microsoft Windows is an operating environment. This means that you still need DOS to use Windows but Windows provides a graphical user interface to use DOS.

---

9. Why are there different versions of operating systems and application software?

ANSWER: Different versions are developed to correct errors in earlier versions and to allow the software to use new technology and hardware devices.

Lesson 8

1. How does application software differ from system software?

ANSWER: System software controls the hardware devices and internal operation of the machine. Applications software allows you to perform certain types of work related tasks.

3. Explain what a cut and paste operation is.

ANSWER: A cut and paste operation deletes text from a document and places the text in a memory area (usually called a clipboard). A paste operation inserts the data in the memory area (clipboard) into a document. The cut and paste operation is used to copy and move data in a document.

5. Data in an electronic spreadsheet are stored in areas called _____. Each one of these storage areas is identified by a _____ letter and a _____ number.

ANSWER: Cells, column, row

7. List the three major database functions and explain what each does.

ANSWER: 1) Storage and Maintenance; allows you to enter and change the database data. 2) Retrieval and Query; allows you to display certain records based upon some criteria. 3) Reporting; allows you to create and print reports with the database data.

9. List several different functions a utility program might perform.

ANSWER: Set alarms, backup files, provide diagnostics, compress and reorganize disks, convert files, create menus, capture screens, blank screens, detect and remove viruses (see table: Common types of Utility Programs).

11. Discuss several questions you should ask before buying software.

ANSWER: Ask what computers the software will run on. Ask how much RAM is required for the program. Ask what processors the program will run. Ask what graphics adapter and operating system is required. Ask about additional hardware required like cables and cards. Ask about the upgrade policy, documentation, and technical support. (see table: Consumer Tips Before Buying Software)

Index

A

add-on board, 33
Alt key, 22
ALU, 39
analog, 101
Apple computers, 51
Apple Macintosh, 10
application software, 120, 126
arithmetic logic unit, 39
ASCII, 41
auto park heads, 88
auto-repeat, 23

B

backup, 89, 93
bar code scanners, 28
BBS, 142
binary digits, 40
binary, 80
bit, 40, 80
bits per second, 103
bksp key, 23
bulletin board, 142
bus LAN, 106
byte, 40, 80
bytes per inch (BPI), 81

C

cache memory, 45
caps lock key, 22
cathode ray tube, 7, 59
CD-ROM, 90
central processing unit, 6, 39
CGA (color graphics adaptor), 60
clip art images, 140
clipboard, 116
clock speed, 41
command driven, 115
compilers, 113
compressed format, 89
Compuserve, 100
computer literacy, 3
    education, 4
    home use, 4
    network, 11
computer privacy, 13
computer viruses, 13
control unit, 39
CPM, 70
CPS, 64
CPU, 6, 39
CRT, 7
Ctrl key, 22
cursor movement keys, 21

D

data bus, 46
data call, 101
data communications, 101
database management system, 135
    key, 136
    query, 136
    storage and maintenance, 135
    reporting, 137
database, 81
del key, 23
demodulate, 102
density, 85
design graphics, 141
desktop publishing, 131
device driver, 24, 58, 74
digital, 101
direct access device, 84
disk drives, 6, 83
diskettes, 6
DOS SHELL, 115
DOS, 115
dot matrix printer, 7, 66
double density, 85
downloading, 104, 141
DPI, 65
draft, 65
drawing pad, 25
drum plotter, 71

Learn PC Computer Literacy